COMPASSION:
THE ULTIMATE ETHIC

Examines and explains the philosophy of veganism, the background to the movement and the practical applications of veganism in everyday life.

W9-BEE-348

COMPASSION
THE ULTIMATE ETHIC

An Exploration of Veganism

by

VICTORIA MORAN

THORSONS PUBLISHERS LIMITED
Wellingborough, Northamptonshire

Produced in co-operation with
The Vegetarian Society of the United Kingdom Ltd.

First published March 1985
Second Impression October 1985

© VICTORIA MORAN 1985

*This book is sold subject to the condition that it shall not, by way of trade or otherwise, be
lent, re-sold, hired out, or otherwise circulated without the publisher's prior consent in any
form of binding or cover other than that in which it is published and without a similar
condition including this condition being imposed on the subsequent purchaser.*

British Library Cataloguing in Publication Data

Moran, Victoria
    Compassion: the ultimate ethic.
    1. Vegetarianism
    I. Title
    613.2'62   RM236

ISBN 0-7225-0953-7

Printed and bound in Great Britain

Contents

	Page
Introduction by Jon Wynne-Tyson	9

Chapter

PART 1
1. The Ultimate Ethic	13
2. Towards A Definition	16
3. Reverence for Life: Schweitzer and Christianity	20
4. Gandhi, Eastern Thought and Ahimsa	27
5. Humans and Other Animals	33
6. The Vegan Stand	37
7. Hunger, Ecology, Peace	45
8. Making the Break	53
9. Nutritional Considerations	61
10. A Holistic Look at Health and Vegans	67
11. The Glorious Possibility	73
Notes to Part 1	75

PART 2
12. Rearing Vegan Children	87
13. Slimming on a Vegan Diet	91
14. Recipes	97
Appendices	106
A. The Vegan Society	107
B. The American Vegan Society	108
C. Vegan Views	109
D. Vegfam	110
E. Miscellaneous Organizations	112
F. The Farm	115
G. Plamil Foods Ltd	117

H.Jane Howard Cosmetics Ltd   119
Selected Bibliography   121
    I. Books and Pamphlets
    II. Other Resources
    III. Additional Recommended Reading
Index   126

Acknowledgements

As I embark upon all the many thank-you's due to numerous people who have made publication of this book possible, I feel moved to start with apologies to those left out. So many people in both England and the United States have been of help on this project that surely not all will be mentioned. Similarly, the Bibliography and Appendices given at the end of this volume cannot be one hundred per cent complete. I know, for example, that there are commercially prepared vegan milks other than Plamil, but I chose that one for inclusion in the appendices since that company was founded by vegans themselves.

It is with vegans themselves, then, that I wish to begin my acknowledgements. I am grateful to Jay and Freya Dinshah who introduced me to this lifestyle in the early 1970s and continue to inspire me. Serena Coles has been of inestimable aid in arranging interviews and agendas on both my research trips to England; and other members of the Vegan Society Council – Kathleen Jannaway, Grace Smith, Eva Batt and the late Jack Sanderson among them – provided valuable assistance. Dr Gill Langley was especially helpful in giving me information for final revisions and, with her husband, Dr Chris Langley, offered welcome hospitality to my husband and me when we were in England. Other British friends who opened their hearts and homes to me during this project include Dr Stephen R. L. Clark and his family, Muriel, the Lady Dowding, Valerie Alferoff and David Barrett of *Vegan Views*, Ruth Howard, Friedenstern and Frances Howard, Margaret Lawson, Marika and Kevin McCartney, Grace Smith, and Jon and Jennifer Wynne-Tyson. Mr Wynne-Tyson deserves special thanks for his Introduction and for presenting this work to the Vegetarian Society for publication consideration.

Father Padraic O. Saori, Christopher Fettes and other members of the Irish Vegetarian Society gave me an enriching view of vegetarianism and veganism in Eire, and the North American Vegetarian Society hosted the conference at which I was able to meet and interview many American vegans. Dr Howard Mueller and Dr William Naumann, professors of mine at North Central College, Naperville, Illinois, were instrumental in my undertaking this project, originally funded by a fellowship from the Richter Foundation. I am also grateful to Mrs Shirley Nicholson of Quest Books who taught me the finer points of book production that made final preparation of the manuscript a far simpler task than it would have been otherwise.

On a more personal level, I wish to thank my husband Patrick Moran who minded the home front during my initial travels and is at this moment rocking our baby while I finish typescript revisions. His honesty, simplicity and continual, unassuming outpouring of compassion in his own life inspire me daily. I want, too, to express appreciation to my parents, Mrs Gladys Marshall and Dr Richard Mucie, who have always encouraged my writing and lovingly accepted my vegetarian leanings; and to Mrs Adelene DeSoto who instilled in me an affection and concern for animals from early childhood. It is my earnest hope to pass this sense of caring on to my daughter Rachael, that she might live in a more humane world.

Introduction
by
Jon Wynne-Tyson

I welcome Victoria Moran's book as an important contribution to holistic health. She sees that holism is a state of affinity and adjustment beyond that of such specific life patterns as a change of diet. While 'dietethics' is a vital facet of the holistic philosophy, it is but an aspect of the whole. But it is a most important aspect, the more so because the nature of what we eat is inextricably bound up with the sum total of human and non-human suffering.

Jeremy Bentham has been quoted (though too seldom) as saying:

The day may come when the rest of the animal creation may acquire those rights which never could have been withheld from them but by the hand of tyranny . . . the question is not can they *reason*? Nor, can they *talk*? But can they *suffer*?

Had he been writing today he might have added that the question was also not whether we can expect to be healthier by abstaining from the flesh and by-products of animals, nor even whether it is more environmentally responsible to eat our plants direct instead of through the bodies of other species, but – for the punchline would have stayed – can they *suffer*?

Because we know that animals can and do suffer – extensively, abominably, incessantly at the hands of our species – the humane argument must always override the rest. Having said which, none of us wishes to be ill, and clearly the argument for vegetarianism is strengthened by evidence that to reduce or abstain from the cruelty implicit in eating other creatures is to enjoy a bonus of improved health.

The specific diseases that may be caused or exacerbated by a diet foreign to the physiology of the upper primates (us) are in these less blinkered times well known to anyone with an eye on the media. In my own and others' books the dietary causes and alleviations of various diseases are discussed. This is not the place for in-depth rehashing of, for example, the relationship between excess cholesterol and heart disease. Suffice it that the evidence (some might add 'and common sense') suggests that a diet as near as possible to that for which man is physically constituted should ensure better physical health and resistance than one giving pride of place to food meant for tigers and hyenas. Contradictions of this rather obvious supposition tend to be unscientific and emotional. Habit does strange things to reason. Some of us like to believe that man is infinitely adaptable, although on every side is stark evidence that this is not so.

It is true, of course, that some of us have lived to what the West regards as a ripe old age despite eating animal products. When these examples are triumphantly produced one asks oneself in what mental and spiritual condition, and to what age, these ancients might have lived had they eaten differently. Probably not as long as those members of the Hunza and other tribes who get into their stride at around 120, but maybe something a little more impressive than the century that brings a telegram from the Queen, or the 106 that competes successfully with the gorier headlines. Yes, all right, I may 'snuff it' at 62, and you may go on to better things at 71 even if you do not switch to apricots and mountain water tomorrow; diet does not have all the answers. But what is less often considered, perhaps because thought unacceptable to the mass readership which is comfortably assumed to want to know what is best for Number One, is whether our participation in the appalling suffering we inflict daily upon countless other sentient beings may be having health consequences reaching beyond specific bodily diseases.

Health is so much more than the absence of physical disease. It is the 'total package' – that of well-being both spiritual and physical and comes from being in tune with our surroundings; in being, so far as possible in this artificial society of ours, in responsible harmony with the rest of life; in proving our voluntary acceptance of those disciplines and standards inseparable from the regimen of the whole (or holistic) man.

I do not limit this observation to that aspect of Holism that is termed Organicism. True health must take account of the spiritual. We cannot enjoy full health if our spiritual nature is at loggerheads with the downpulling and devolutionary demands of our physical being. Conflict is the antithesis of health, and conflict is present in any state of imbalance. There is no balance in the nature that is not true to itself. The frenzied attempts at self-justification that can result from the effort to live on two different levels must take their toll. Where the mind knows that the stomach should heed the heart rather than habit, there is conflict. When the mind has seen the evidence of the indivisibility of cruelty, the indivisibility of rights, and the evils of what has been called 'speciesism', it can only invite conflict by rejecting those changes of habits that must follow honest consideration of the implications of that realization.

Health, then, is not just a matter of what we eat, what drugs and pollution we avoid, where we live, and how much leisure we enjoy. It is also a matter of stress, and stress is something not produced only by uncongenial work, inharmonious relationships, and the imposed strains of modern life, but also by the awareness, however deeply buried, that we are not living as compassionately and as responsibly as our hearts and minds, given reign, tell us we should be living.

As Dr Catherine Roberts wrote in her fine book *The Scientific Conscience*, 'Man's increasing awareness of humaneness indicates that he has reached a new threshold in his evolution.' If we damp down that awareness, if we argue against our own instincts and against reason – as we have to do in order to justify the sins of cruelty and callous indifference to others' suffering – then we are doing ourselves the greater harm.

No species that fights against evolutionary prompting is going to flourish. True health resides in that feeling for life, for the unity of being, that enables the whole man to function to the limit of his understanding and perceptions. I think we ignore this 'fact of life' at our present and future peril.

I believe Victoria Moran points up all that I have tried to say in this brief introduction, and a great many other wise and helpful things besides.

Part 1

1.

The Ultimate Ethic

When I was in London to do the greater part of my research on veganism, a film called *Meetings With Remarkable Men* was playing in Knightsbridge. I did not see it but I believe I lived its name. In meetings with vegans in Great Britain (where veganism began as an organized movement) and Ireland, and later in the United States, I was indeed contacting remarkable men and women. They are unique in two ways. First, they espouse an extended code of ethics, believing that the Golden Rule applies not only to our conduct with fellow humans but to the animal kingdom and, inasmuch as is possible, to the plant world and the earth itself. Secondly, they do not imprison their ideals in emotional or intellectual cells but act on them daily.

This is most apparent at the dinner table since 'For most humans, especially those in modern urban and suburban communities, the most direct form of contact with non-human animals is at meal time: we eat them.'[1] The vegan not only refuses to eat the animals, but he does not eat anything *from* an animal, such as eggs or dairy produce. Furthermore, he does not cease being vegan between meals: there are numerous other consumer goods and pastimes which he believes to be the direct result of some form of pain or exploitation and from which he therefore abstains. The exhaustive list of such things – including silk, wool, feather pillows, boar brushes, ivory, certain perfumes, toiletries and household cleaning products, most drugs, fishing, dog and horse racing, circuses and animal acts – does not tell the vegan that he is fanatical or impractical. It rather illustrates the staggering extent to which Western society depends upon objects and amusements which he believes to be immoral and which he has proved to his own satisfaction to be unnecessary.

I must reveal at the outset that I am not writing in the impartial, objective style of the pure scholar. Knowing vegans has convinced me of their sensibility and consistency. I admire their philosophy, approve of their convictions, and cannot find a single crack in their logic. This puts me in a similar position to Dr Stephen Clark's when he states early in his book *The Moral Status of Animals*, 'I am a committed crank and a zoophile, and my hope is to convert my audience.'[2]

Who is ripe for such conversion? 'That', a British vegan of twenty years' standing told me, borrowing some American currency, 'is the $64,000 question!' The vegans I met represent the full spectrum of social, economic, professional and educational backgrounds. Their age range is wide and males and females number equally in their ranks. Although I cannot make educated sociological or psychological assessments, I can report as a layperson that no 'personality type' is apparent. These people seem to have developed their potential for compassion to a great degree, in rather the way a wine taster or perfume tester has developed one of his physical senses. I did not find vegans to be weak, emotional or hypersensitive as some critics have intimated, nor completely selfless, totally courageous or generally bordering on saintly. They are human beings with human failings, although they are exceptionally caring, thoughtful and consistent. This book, however, concentrates on the vegan way of life as ethics in practice rather than on individual vegans. If they were some special breed, their movement would have little purpose other than as a social outlet for people who drink nut milk and make soufflés out of soya beans. On the contrary, by living his life, the vegan shows that health, contentment and productivity are enhanced by what he believes to be an ethos of enlightened morality.

My aim is to present the lifestyle as a spiritual adventure, although it can be considered religious only in the broadest sense of that term. The people I interviewed come from myriad religious traditions and many remain active as Christians or members of other organized faiths; some are avowed atheists. Most of the vegans I met in both Britain and America are not allied with a particular church but feel, as one expressed it, 'My life is my religion.' Albert Schweitzer worded it well when he said, 'Thought becomes religious when it thinks itself out to the end.'[3]

Freedom of thought and differences of opinion are legion

among vegans, yet they stand firm in their basic convictions: harmlessness and reverence for life, and compassion as the ultimate ethic, the spirit of *ahimsa*. That Sanskrit word for non-killing and non-injury may be viewed in vast scope as 'dynamic harmlessness', as purposefully living to do the most good as well as the least harm possible. *Ahimsa* is, in fact, the title of the American Vegan Society's membership journal. This East Indian term is one of the 'limbs of yoga' and was borrowed from its Hindu parent to become an integral aspect of Buddhism and the very soul of Jainism. Therefore, I mistakenly assumed that Eastern thought would have strongly influenced nearly all vegans. This is true in some cases, but the Society of Friends and its pacifism have possibly influenced more of them. A few mentioned Thoreau, Teilhard de Chardin or Gandhi, but the overwhelming impression I received in five weeks' concentrated contact with vegans on two continents was that they are vegan because, to them, it is simply and obviously right. They seem to share an inner knowledge of this rightness that does not depend upon a common background of rearing or reading.

Therefore, although I will present religious, philosophical and literary support for the vegans' approach, I do not propose that these writings necessarily influenced great numbers of people to adopt this lifestyle. 'Vegans are just ordinary people', Kathleen Jannaway, former Secretary of The (British) Vegan Society, told me, 'who, often at great inconvenience to themselves, do something just for disinterested compassion. They do gain, though, both in health of body and, if they've been sensitive, freedom of mind. It brings great liberation of spirit to feel you're not causing suffering.'

2.

Towards a Definition

If *Dorland's Medical Dictionary* were the definitive source on the subject at hand, my task of examining veganism would be relatively simple. According to *Dorland's*, a vegan is 'an extreme vegetarian who excludes all animal protein from his diet'.[1] Of course, that dictionary also phoneticizes the word as 'vej'an' while everyone who is such, including those in England who coined the term in the early 1940s, pronounce it 'vee'gan'. There are conflicting reports on the word's origin. American Vegan Society literature has said that it is derived from the Spanish *vega* which means 'plain', the source of vegans' food. But the story in England is that one of the Vegan Society's founders, Donald Watson, wearied of writing 'total vegetarian' and used the first three and the final two letters of 'vegetarian' since veganism starts there and carries vegetarianism through to its logical conclusion.

It is true, then, that vegans are vegetarians, the 'real' ones, some would say. A vegetarian – that word, by the way, is derived from the Latin *vegetus* meaning 'full of life', not from 'vegetable'[2] – is one who consumes no flesh, fish or fowl. He may use dairy products and would then technically be a 'lacto-vegetarian', or eggs (an 'ovo-vegetarian'), or both, in which case he would belong to the largest segment of the non-meat-eating population, that of 'lacto-ovo-vegetarians'. The so-called 'ethical vegetarian', one who chooses a meatless diet out of concern for the animals bred and killed for food rather than from considerations of personal health or economics,[3] may also wish to avoid slaughterhouse by-products such as leather and certain drug and cosmetic ingredients. He would also be likely to oppose intensive ('battery' or 'factory') husbandry methods, vivisection, hunting, the wearing of furs, etc., as would the vegan. None of these considerations, though, would make a person a vegetarian – many animal activists eat meat – or keep him from being one. Vegans are generally regarded as non-dairy-and-egg-eating vegetarians, 'concerned with the cruelty, exploitation and slaughter involved by the human consumption of animal food.'[4] Even so, veganism is not simply a dietary issue.

Just as one may be a vegetarian yet see no need for going on to veganism, one may be on a vegan diet and still use non-food products, or participate in events, that the vegan would regard as exploitative. There are, for example, numerous health teachings (such as those of the Natural Hygiene Societies) that encourage a diet free from all animal foods, yet do not migrate from their sphere of influence to comment on the plight of laboratory animals or the morality of a bullfight. Many medical doctors, cardiologists in particular, have found it impossible to ignore the increasing body of evidence in their professional journals attesting to the value of a completely plant-based dietary. They advise their patients to clear the meat out of the freezer, outgrow their milk habit, and feed any eggs in the refrigerator to the dog, who has a much higher tolerance for dietary cholesterol than does a human. These doctors are not telling anyone to give his leather shoes to charity or to replace his shampoo with one that has not been injected into rabbits' eyes.[5] Even if this were part of the prescription, its being carried out would not make one a vegan in the way I shall be using the term because the *decision* to enlarge the individual's horizons of compassion would be lacking.

It is true that one may become a vegetarian or a 'dietary vegan' for the motive of better health and as a result tap latent springs of loving concern within himself which bring him to veganism in both spirit and action. An example of that is my husband, who turned vegetarian as he researched his graduate thesis in physiology on the effect of animal foods on the cardio-vascular system. In the nine years since, he has gradually replaced worn-out shoes and belts with non-leather ones, almost eliminated dairy products, and actually made a career change (he had trained to become a teacher of biology), based in part on his growing aversion to animal use and abuse in science courses. The development of the compassionate sense appears to be progressive.

Even within the organizational structure of The Vegan Society, established in England in 1944, a progression of objectives is evidenced. Its original aims, as listed in a 1946 issue of its quarterly, *The Vegan*, were:

1. To advocate that man's food should be derived from fruits, nuts, vegetables, grains and other wholesome non-animal products and that it should exclude flesh, fish, fowl, eggs, honey and animals' milk, butter, and cheese.

2. To encourage the manufacture and use of alternatives to animal commodities.[6]

By 1947, a third aim had been added:

To extend and organize Veganism nationally and internationally and to facilitate contacts between those following the Vegan Way of Life.[7]

(That point on facilitating contacts is still important: it is imperative to understand that veganism is not dependent upon membership in any organization, and many vegans – perhaps most when considered on the international level – have no such affiliation.)

After twenty years in existence, The Vegan Society[8] revised its three points into a succinct – and, I would submit, 'progressively compassionate' – statement of purpose:

Veganism is a way of living which excludes all forms of exploitation of, and cruelty to, the animal kingdom, and includes a reverence and compassion for all life. It applies to the practice of living on the products of the plant kingdom to the exclusion of flesh, fish, fowl, eggs, honey, animal milk and its derivatives, and encourages the use of alternatives for all commodities derived wholly or in part from animals.

Veganism remembers man's responsibilities to the earth and its resources and seeks to bring about a healthy soil and plant kingdom and a proper use of the materials of the earth.[9]

The 1980 statement had evolved still further:

Veganism is a way of living on the products of the plant kingdom to the exclusion of flesh, fish, fowl, eggs, animal milk and its derivatives (the taking of honey being left to individual conscience).[10] It encourages the study and use of alternatives for all commodities normally derived wholly or partly from animals.

The objects of The Vegan Society are to further knowledge of, and interest in, sound nutrition and in the vegan method of agriculture and food production as a means of increasing the potential of the earth to the physical, moral and economic advantage of mankind.[11]

This historical sampling of quotations indicates a non-static movement. It also makes the formulation of a full and accurate definition of veganism beyond the terse one given in the medical dictionary quite difficult. Nevertheless, a summary sentence from *Why Veganism?* by Eva Batt, onetime Secretary of The Vegan Society, provides the understanding from which I shall be working: 'Veganism is one thing and one thing only – a way of living which avoids exploitation, whether it be of our fellow men, the animal population, or the soil upon which we rely for our very existence.'[12]

3.
Reverence For Life:
Schweitzer and Christianity

Albert Schweitzer built a philosophy around 'reverence for life', a philosophy which both germinated and came to fruition within his Christian theology. 'Reverence for Life', he wrote, 'affords me my fundamental principle that good consists in maintaining, assisting and enhancing life, and that to destroy, to harm or to hinder life is evil.'[1] Although not himself a vegan, Schweitzer was in contact at least once with the American Vegan Society to which he communicated,

I am conscious that flesh-eating is not in accordance with the finer feelings and I abstain from it whenever I can . . . It belongs to the characteristics of Man to be kind and compassionate to all creatures. . . I am convinced that the destiny of Man is, to become more and more humane.[2]

Schweitzer's 'fundamental principle' is pivotal to veganism. It was in fact the motivating factor for people who adopted the vegan lifestyle long before it was so named and before the world knew of the physician/musician/theologian ministering in Lambarene. A committed vegan lives reverence for life whether he has met with the works of Schweitzer or not. (I am reminded of a friend who helped a stranded motorist and was told gratefully, 'This is such a Christian thing for you to do!' Actually, my friend is Jewish, not Christian, but he understood the intent.) Schweitzer was not the first to isolate this ethical precept, but he polished it like a diamond and presented it in a mounting custom-crafted for the modern West.

No sentimentalist, he realized that 'The world is indeed the grisly drama of will-to-live at variance with itself.'[3] He was keenly aware, however, of his cognizance as a human being of this 'will-to-live' in entities outside himself, *homo sapiens* and otherwise. Taking responsibility for a sacrificed life taken to preserve a presumably greater form is central to his thought, but preceding this is the need to be certain that taking life, even that of a plant, is really called for. The story is told of the good doctor's reacting almost in horror to the suggestion that he take a shortcut through a field while walking with a friend. To walk on earth when pavement was available would have meant the avoidable death of many insects whose lives were to Schweitzer a more important consideration than his saving a little time.[4]

In practice, Schweitzer's acting out of reverence for life differed somewhat from the vegans'. Most of them, for example, are strict anti-vivisectionists while Schweitzer, although he criticized pointless and repetitive animal experiments, was a medical doctor who supported limited use of animals in laboratories. The *moral foundation* for their choices, however, is identical:

> Just as in my own will-to-live there is a yearning for more life, and of that mysterious exaltation of the will-to-live which is called pleasure . . . so the same obtains in all the will-to-live around me . . .
>
> Ethics consist in this, that I experience the necessity of practicing the same reverence for life toward all will-to-live, as toward my own.[5]

The vegans I have studied came to this moral destination via many routes. Schweitzer reached it on a Christian path, believing as he did that 'The ethic of reverence for life is the ethic of Jesus brought into philosophical expression, extended into cosmical form, and conceived as intellectually necessary.'[6]

Perhaps because we as humans do not generally extend things 'into cosmical form', the Christian message has not been a major one for influencing potential vegans. There are exceptions to this, though. One such is Margaret Lawson, founder of the 'Fellowship of Life', an organization which seeks to prod clergy into recognition of animal welfare issues. She became a 'committed Christian' at the age of 9 and later a 'consecrated Christian' and a pacifist. '"Thou shalt not kill" rang in my ears for a fortnight,' she related at her home, also a vegan/vegetarian guesthouse, in northern Scotland.

> Suddenly it struck me that that should include animals as well and I stopped eating meat. I knew no vegetarians and didn't know if this was practical; I went to the [Church of Scotland] minister for help and was shocked that he wouldn't help me.

I wanted to be vegan from the start. 'Thou shalt not kill' set me to want to give up the whole business, but I was advised to give my body a chance to change so I was lacto-vegetarian for eighteen months. When I did turn vegan, I didn't even think about it; I just didn't want anything to do with animal food.[7]

The phrase that sparked Mrs Lawson's change in lifestyle came, to be sure, from the Jewish tradition that predated Christianity. For her and others who see support for their vegetarianism/veganism in that commandment, a translator's note that 'kill' should read 'murder' is irrelevant. Just as a pacifist regards killing in war as murder, so do vegans see killing animals for food, fashion or sport as a murderous activity.

Other Old Testament quotations come up in discussions with Jewish and Christian vegans and vegetarians. The original diet for man given in Genesis 1:29 is often cited: 'And God said, "Behold, I have given you every herb bearing seed, which is upon the face of the earth, and every tree, in the which is the fruit of a tree yielding seed; to you it shall be for meat."' Later exceptions to this came, say vegetarians, as temporary or emergency measures only. Animals were not forgotten by God when Hosea spoke for Him, 'In that day will I make a covenant for them with the beasts of the field and with the fowls of heaven and with the creeping things of the ground, and I will break the bow and the sword and the battle out of the land and make them lie down safely' (Hosea 2:18). The prophecy of Isaiah 11:9, 'They shall not hurt nor destroy in All My Holy Mountain' is another favourite (it appears on the cover of the Fellowship of Life pamphlet *Calling All Christians*) as is Isaiah 11:6: 'The wolf also shall dwell with the lamb, and the leopard shall lie down with the kid; and the calf and the young lion and the fatling together, and a little child shall lead them.' That last phrase is important since some vegans believe that humans must lead the way in a planetary progression of advancing humaneness. This is to truly have 'dominion' as caretakers and guides for 'younger' creatures sharing in an evolutionary journey (shades of Teilhard de Chardin here).

Attention is also drawn by some to the Hebrew prophets' decrying ritual sacrifices. The vegan might submit that at least part of the reason why an Amos or Micah opposed these so vehemently was because of the animal suffering involved. Skipping some centuries, Jesus' cleansing of the Temple was pointed out to me as an act of saving potential sacrifice victims as well as reconsecrating a holy site.

Even so, I contacted few vegans who are Biblical literalists and none whose veganism rests on the Bible alone. All are well aware that persuasive arguments for all manner of animal abuse may be – and have been – drawn from Scripture, just as the case for slavery was defended with a militia of Testamental verbatims of both Old and New variety. Such inconsistencies do not seem to trouble vegans. Those who are professing Jews or Christians give personal liberality in scriptural interpretation, mistaken translating, or 'layers of meaning' in all holy books as reasons why they are not bothered by lack of total Biblical back-up for their views.

A query I made of nearly all the vegans I met was, 'How do you respond to the statement, "Jesus ate fish"?' Margaret Lawson said simply, 'If Jesus were the person he was supposed to have been, he'd have lived up to Genesis 1:29 and Isaiah 11:9. There were vegetarians in his time and he'd have to have known about them.' (The vegetarians in his time usually brought up by those in our time are the Essenes, the Jewish sect often linked to John the Baptist and sometimes, with less evidence, to Christ himself. A substantial proportion of the vegans questioned simply accept that both were Essenes and leave it at that.) 'Jesus must at least have been aware of the Essenes,' according to Kathleen Jannaway, a Quaker.

If he weren't vegetarian, he wasn't the sort of man I thought he was . . . The only time in the Gospels he was said to eat anything of animal origin was after the Resurrection. What sort of body was that? We just don't know . . . They love to show pictures of Jesus with a lamb. Can you think of his cutting its throat?

A young wife and mother (from Holland, living in London) accepts that he ate fish but 'I trust he would not eat it if he were a close friend of mine now.' A 21-year-old British student excused Jesus since 'he probably didn't know any better,' and his girlfriend, eighteen, took a historical view: 'In his time it was extreme to ask people not to kill or torture each other; his teachings were as advanced for his time as ours are now.' An American Baptist woman gave virtually the same response, adding that '2,000 years later, we should be ready to extend his loving concept to all creatures.'

Vegans who are not Christians were generally disinterested

in the entire issue ('Eating fish may have been his choice; I choose not to harm others,' was a typical response), but a few used the fish problem to substantiate anti-Christianity feelings. There were some answers like, 'That proves he wasn't as holy as he thought he was,' and 'His eating fish doesn't shock me since much of Christianity appears to be based on violence.' It is true that of the vegans I met, not many practise as orthodox Christians. Even Margaret Lawson, spurred on as she was by 'Thou shalt not kill', said,

I would describe myself now as a universalist. I've tried to get a word for this but I can't. 'Mystic' doesn't describe it either because you can be a mystic without being there ... There is a stage further than being a consecrated Christian, when even Jesus falls out and there is only God.

This is not to imply that Christianity and concern for non-humans are necessarily incompatible. There are in both England and Ireland active Catholic Study Circles for Animal Welfare; the Friends (Quaker) Vegetarian Society (see Appendix E) and Quaker Concern for Animal Welfare have worked in this arena since the turn of the century. Dean Carpenter of Westminster is a vegetarian and chairman of the Christian Consultative Council for Animal Welfare, a joint body of different denominations working for the betterment of animals through the churches. Nevertheless, Christianity as usually interpreted has not historically fostered sufficient concern for animal life to prompt many to take the major step of veganism, and the Church's record on animal issues generally has not been a glowing one. The late Revd V. A. Holmes-Gore, an Anglican clergyman, lamented,

If we seek examples of men who have shown a Christ-like tenderness towards the creatures, we shall often find them among the heretics, the pagans and the agnostics ... It is true that many of those whom the Church afterwards canonized were 'animal lovers', but they had no influence upon the Church's teaching or attitude to the creatures.[8]

In traditional Christian theology, animals have been regarded as non-moral beings since only man is created in the 'image of God'. Humankind has been further separated from other sentient beings by the 'dominion' idea. This led early theologians such as Aquinas to conclude that an animal could have no 'immortal soul', thus possessing no rights and having no inherent value outside its usefulness to man.[9] Since, according to Thomism, animals are intended for man's use, nothing he can do to them, including taking their lives, can be considered wrong.[10] Those who have been led to a fuller appreciation of reverence for life through Christian teachings would take more of the view suggested by Paul in Romans 8:19 and following verses, in which he alludes to the whole natural order's awaiting rescue from its suffering.

The apostle tells his fellow Christians that they themselves have a vital role in redeeming creation and this is part of their stewardship. Christ through his death and resurrection has restored to us and to our fellow creatures the hope of fulfilment 'to enter upon the liberty and splendour of the sons of God'.

Nothing less than Paul's vision should guide our thinking on animal rights, and this is why I say that in the past animal rights have been poorly served by moral theologians.[11]

Indeed, few sermons have been preached on the plight of animals, possibly because of the misconception that to care for them would dilute our interest in the needs of people. Father Padraig O. Saorai, C. C., chairman of the Irish Catholic Study Circle for Animal Welfare, called that '. . . ridiculous! Caring is a natural progression – for the country you live in . . . animals . . . your fellow human beings. It's almost a chain reaction.' The Study Circle sees that although the Catholic Church has not 'as yet officially proclaimed a mandatory moral code of behaviour towards animals . . . the Church is constantly growing in its deeper understanding of the Christian message.'[12] This 'deeper understanding' may be reflected in Father Saorai's concept of the heart of Christian teachings as 'Love everybody; be kind to animals; and respect all life because all life is sacred.' Amazingly similar to this view is the definition of 'true religion' given by Stephen Gaskin, founder and spiritual leader of The Farm (see Appendix F), a vegan community some 500 strong in the rural American village of Summertown, Tennessee. According to Gaskin, 'true religion is based on compassion, doesn't exclude anybody, helps you in the here and now, and doesn't cost anything.'[13]

Just as compassion can philosophically connect a Dublin priest and a Tennessee guru, it has been a curious point of similarity in otherwise dissimilar Christian groups. Some Roman Catholic orders, notably the Trappists, the Poor Clare

Sisters, and certain Carmelites, have adhered to a vegetarian diet. Using a Biblical and hygienic basis, about half of Seventh Day Adventists are vegetarian and in this group are dietary vegans. Some Mormons find a vegetarian and even vegan diet suggested by their scriptures, although most interpret the teachings as recommending meat-eating in moderation. The Mormon *Word of Wisdom* states, 'And it is pleasing to me that they [meat and poultry] should not be used, only in times of winter, or of cold, or of famine.'

The Order of the Cross and the Followers of the Way are two spiritual groups based on the teachings of Todd Ferrier, a one-time Congregational clergyman who died in 1943. His unique insights into Christianity show vegetarianism as a crucial prerequisite to true Christian living, and many of his followers have expanded this in their own lives to veganism. Other groups which have suggested vegetarianism to their members are those which are Christian but have accepted varying degrees of Far Eastern influence. These include the Rosicrucian Fellowship, the Anthroposophical Society, the Liberal Catholic Church (no connection with the Roman Catholic Church), and the Unity School of Christianity. 'The great need of the popular form of the Christian religion is precisely a belief in the solidarity of all living things,' wrote Dr Anna Kingsford, a theosophist dedicated to 'esoteric Christianity' and a champion of animal rights in the late nineteenth century. 'It is in this that Buddhism surpasses Christianity – in this divine recognition of the universal right to charity.'[14] It is fitting, then, to move from Schweitzer's base in Christianity to Eastern religious thought, the idea of *ahimsa* and its modern spokesman, Mahatma Gandhi.

4.

Gandhi, Eastern Thought and Ahimsa

The paradoxical nature of the Gandhi phenomenon provokes a certain fascination: a tiny man but a great one; a David to the Goliath of imperialism yet a David with no material weapon, not even a slingshot; an educated and eminently literate man identified with the common people, bread labour and the weaving of *khadi*; one intent upon feeding and freeing others, but who spent long periods fasting in gaol; a person revered by many as a modern saint but who felt in ceaseless conflict with his own 'lower self', and a devout Hindu who nevertheless could embrace all the religions of the world. Gandhi's vegetarianism is common knowledge, and he is often remembered as accompanied by the she-goat who provided him with milk. Less widely realized, though, is that the Mahatma was at heart a vegan and in 1931 called his dependence upon goat's milk 'the tragedy of his life'.[1] His physicians nevertheless deemed its use necessary to his health due to a digestive system impaired by youthful over-indulgence in the pungent curries of his homeland and excessive fasting for political reasons later. He reluctantly complied with the doctors' orders but wrote:

I believe that in the limitless vegetable kingdom there is an effective substitute for milk, which, every medical man admits, has its drawbacks and which is destined by Nature not for man, but for babies and young ones of lower animals. I should count no cost too dear for making a search.[2]

In these days of commercial plant milks, soya dairies and electric blenders, 'effective substitutes' are readily available, although public demand for them is still not widespread.

But why should cows and nanny goats have mattered to

Gandhi, surrounded as he was by the poverty and squalor of *people* in his beloved India? The answer may lie in his immersion in the doctrine of *ahimsa* and his inability to limit its call for 'dynamic harmlessness' to his own species alone. From his writings comes:

> To see the universal and all-pervading Spirit of Truth face to face, one must be able to love the meanest of creation as oneself . . .
>
> The only means for realization of Truth is *Ahimsa* . . . [It] is not the crude thing it has been made to appear. Not to hurt any living thing is no doubt a part of *Ahimsa*, but it is its least expression. The principle of *Ahimsa* is hurt by every evil thought, by undue haste, by lying, by hatred, by wishing ill to anybody.[3]

When asked if he would kill a cobra in self-defence, he replied that for him to do so would be to violate his vows both of non-killing and of fearlessness, that he would try to inwardly calm the snake with loving vibrations, thereby not lowering his ideals to ease a frightening situation. 'With his charming candour he added, "I must confess that I could not serenely carry on this conversation were I faced by a cobra!"'[4] Even so, Gandhi was familiar with the aphorism on *ahimsa* in Patanjali's *Yoga Sutras*: 'When a man becomes steadfast in his abstention from harming others, then all living creatures will cease to feel enmity in his presence.'[5]

Patanjali was not alone among the Indian ancients to include *ahimsa* as an important religious precept. The *Bhagavad-Gita* (so inspirational to Gandhi despite its military imagery which he accepted as simply that – imagery) is replete with references to the *ahimsa* ideal. Every action of the enlightened person is said to be 'wed to the welfare of fellow creatures'.[6] Lord Krishna affirms in the poetry of the *Gita*, 'That yogi . . . is established in union with me, who worships me devoutly in all beings . . . Who burns with the bliss and suffers the sorrow of every creature . . . Him I hold highest of all the yogis;'[7] and 'A man should not hate any living creature. Let him be friendly and compassionate to all.'[8] The epic *Mahabarata* also stresses *ahimsa* and refers to it as *sakalo dharma*, 'virtue entire', not simply abstention from injurious practices but with the understanding that to refrain from helping others in some way hurts them.[9]

Ahimsa need not, however, be filed under 'H' for Hinduism. It is in the theology of Jainism, indeed a Hindu offspring, that *ahimsa* is elevated to its highest place among world religions. A sect that values asceticism, Jainism summarizes its aims in the 'Five Great Vows' given for monks. The first vow is, '. . . I renounce all killing of living beings . . . Nor shall I myself kill living beings or cause others to do it, nor consent to it . . .'[10] Those who know little else of Jainism are familiar with the monks' placing gauze over their noses and mouths lest they breathe in an insect. The faith has been criticized for inconsistency: Jains will not farm, for example, due to the unavoidable killing of bugs and worms in the process, yet they purchase produce others have raised. Still, the philosophical undergirding of *ahimsa* expressed by Jainism's founder, Lord Mahavira, is firm:

All living beings love their life, desire pleasure, and are averse to pain; they dislike any injury to themselves; everybody is desirous of life, and to every being, his own life is very dear . . .

This is the quintessence of wisdom: Not to injure any living being.[11]

It was not Jainism, though, but Buddhism that was mentioned most often by those vegans who believed that the tenets of some religion come close to vegan principles.[12] This is not surprising since Buddhism calls itself the way of compassion. Among Mahayana Buddhist proverbs, for example, is found: 'Abstinence from eating and killing [animate creatures] is already a Bodhisattvahood [in becoming].'[13] Gautama is reported in the *Dhammapada* to have said, 'A man is not noble if he injures living creatures' and in the *Lankavatara Sutra*:

To avoid causing terror to living beings, let the Disciple refrain from eating meat . . . There may be some foolish people in the future who will say that I permitted meat-eating and that I partook of meat myself, but . . . meat-eating in any form, in any manner, and in any place, is unconditionally prohibited for all.[14]

Not only is vegetarianism stressed in the *Surangama Sutra* ('Those who eat meat . . . will never attain enlightenment') but – for the monks – veganism is asked:

Disciples, if they are true and sincere, will not wear garments of silk, nor wear boots constructed of leather, because it involves the destruction of life. Disciples will not ingest products of milk or cheese because thereby they are depriving young animals of that which rightly belongs to them.[15]

Again, these admonitions are not universally heeded – the monks' humble acceptance of whatever is placed in their begging bowls is well-known – but they are 'on the books' just as loving one's neighbour as oneself is central to Christian ethics whether all Christians reach that ideal or not. This love for fellow man is an outgrowth of the Christian idea that all people are children of one heavenly Father. In Far Eastern thought, all creatures are seen as manifestations of God. Even though the human is the highest form of life on earth and it is in this embodiment that one is believed to be able to reach knowledge of and union with God:

We are a part of the single organic whole, which is life. This is the very basis of spiritual vegetarianism . . .

When you see an animal, the idea of brotherhood should arise in you; if it doesn't, you should work to cultivate that feeling.[16]

From that beginning, it is believed that further understanding – i.e. of people – can grow. It does seem easier to behave without malice towards a dumb and docile creature than towards another person whose words and wants are apt to collide with one's own. Perhaps it is for this reason that H. Jay Dinshah, founder of the American Vegan Society, chose 'Abstinence from Animal Products' as the first of six 'Pillars of Ahimsa'.[17] This is not simply the prejudice of a man who agrees with the notion. 'Abstention from animal food' is given by Hardon in *Religions of the Orient, a Christian View*, in no way a vegetarian-oriented text, as the first practical application of *ahimsa*, followed by 'pacifism . . . [and] regarding all living beings as kindred.'[18] The vegetarian view of that kinship is as straightforward as a tee-shirt appliquéd with 'Animals are my friends and I don't eat my friends'. The vegan goes beyond this in remembering that *ahimsa* is not just non-killing but non-injury as well. To prematurely separate a cow from her calf in order to provide milk for marketing, to keep hens in the deplorable conditions of the modern 'battery', or to subject the civet cat to repeated scrapings of the penis to obtain a fixative for perfume, are practices repugnant to the vegan, although none of them involves immediate killing.

Eventual slaughter comes, of course: laying hens provide casseroles; the gentle cow is recycled into hamburger when her lactation wanes, and any male calves she produced were long since trucked off to veal units. In this era of artificial

insemination, super-ovulation and embryo transfer, few bulls
are needed for breeding. Half the Holsteins in the state of
Pennsylvania today, as an example, are descended from the
same sire, one 'Osborndale Ivanhoe' who, though dead
seventeen years, continued to father dairy cattle post-mortem.[19]
That particular animal was sufficiently spectacular to avoid the
slaughterhouse and is actually buried, complete with a tomb-
stone, outside the laboratory that houses his sperm ('We'll
never bury another one . . . There's no profit in that'[20]). Even
so, the vegan would see his years of confinement, his subjection
to the electrical shocks of the 'electro-ejaculator', and man's
general meddling in the genetics of another species as totally
unacceptable.

The desire of non-vegans who are concerned about animals
is for a return to traditional agricultural methods, but population
numbers and urban/suburban centralization put this hope,
say vegans, in the pipe dream category. There is work being
done to better the lot of animals in intensive farming situations
and to legislate for more humane conditions; one of the most
successful groups dedicated to this is the English organization
'Compassion in World Farming'. Its founder Peter Roberts,
however, is himself a vegan, the consensus among whom is
that *ahimsa* can only be practised fully via a gradual cessation in
the demand for animal goods of all kinds.

Dinshah's second 'pillar' is 'Harmlessness with Reverence
for Life'. *Ahimsa* is seen as an ideal and one attempts to reach
that. It does not mean that a person can live and never do any
harm at all (i.e. killing no plants or microbes) but actions are to
be weighed carefully. Reverence for life is not animal worship
but respect for life itself.

Man must get his thoughts, words and actions out of this vast moral
jungle. We are not predators. We are, hopefully, more than
instinctive killers and selfish brutes. Why take such a dim view of our
potentials and capabilities?[21]

Pillar number three is 'Integrity of Thought, Word and Deed',
calling for humility and the harmony of one's thinking,
speaking and acting. By practising veganism, one who believes
in *ahimsa* puts his life in tune with his logic and saves himself
mental turmoil. 'Mastery Over Oneself', the conquest of one's
lower nature in order to realize the higher, is the fourth pillar,
and 'Service to Mankind, Nature and Creation' the fifth. This

service is seen as the 'path of duty' by which non-violent people, when they have the courage to live by their ideals and set examples for others, can win the world for love, peace and harmony. 'Advancement of Understanding and Truth' completes the support structure in Dinshah's view of *ahimsa*:

Man cannot pretend to be higher in ethics, spirituality, advancement, or civilization than other creatures and at the same time live by lower standards than the vulture or hyena . . .

The Pillars of Ahimsa indisputably represent the clearest, surest path out of the jungle, and toward the attainment of that highly desirable goal.[22]

But does it work? Is *ahimsa* practical and applicable, or is it a philosophical abstraction that might capture the fancy of only the occasional idealist? Any traveller to India would attest, by way of example, that cows there may be sacred but they're also very thin. Where is all this *ahimsa?* Was its moment of glory over with Gandhi's leading India in her struggle for national self-determination?

He fought with Hindu weapons – non-violent resistance, soul-force, a baffling use of tolerance and inclusive good will when confronted with strong opposition . . . with astonishing practicality as to means but unyielding idealism in matters of principle.[23]

The ideal, however, whether connected with the word *ahimsa*, some other word or no word at all, has guided other thinkers of the East and West throughout the centuries; and these thinkers, almost to a man, have been 'doers' as well. Today, one sees facets of *ahimsa* operating in non-violent social change, human and animal welfare groups, among ethical vegetarians and many others, but it is in the vegan movement that this ethic reigns supreme.

5.

Humans and Other Animals

Dr Martin Luther King is a recent exponent of *ahimsa* in the West. The results of his tireless work are evident in racial equality in the United States, light years beyond its status when he began his peaceable campaign, despite the fact that the task he started remains unfinished. What had been called Gandhi's 'Hindu weapons' were Dr King's Christian implements. He urged in 1964,

Some of you have knives, and I ask you to put them up. Some of you have arms, and I ask you to put them up. Get the weapon of nonviolence, the breastplate of righteousness, the armour of truth and just keep on marching.[1]

Although King was not a vegetarian himself, he unwittingly influenced others in that direction. Probably the most famous example of this is comedian/crusader Dick Gregory who turned vegetarian in 1965.

The philosophy of nonviolence which I learned from Dr Martin Luther King, Jr., during my involvement in the civil rights movement was first responsible for my change in diet.

. . . Under the leadership of Dr King, I became totally committed to nonviolence, and I was convinced that nonviolence meant opposition to killing in any form. I felt the commandment 'Thou shalt not kill' applied to human beings not only in their dealings with each other – war, lynching, assassination, murder and the like – but in their practice of killing animals for food or sport. Animals suffer and die alike. Violence causes the same pain . . . the same arrogant, cruel and brutal taking of life.[2]

This connection was not a revelation of the 1960s. Numerous great men of the past were vegetarian. (Presumably, great women were as well, although information on their habits, dietary and otherwise, has not been as well-preserved.) Some of these were surely vegan: living in simpler times, they must have looked to nature and realized that no 'lacto-carnivores' or 'lacto-vegetarians' exist there, that man alone refuses to be weaned. In any case, the list of such people is impressive, including as it does Plutarch, Porphyry, Sir Isaac Newton, Jean Jacques Rousseau, Richard Wagner, Alexander Pope, Susan B. Anthony, Annie Besant,[3] and more recently Isaac Bashevis Singer and Helen and Scott Nearing. Someone always adds Adolf Hitler since it has been reported that he was vegetarian for several years in hopes of relieving a persistent stomach complaint. He maintained, however, a 'weakness for meat-filled ravioli, and was especially fond of the sausage to be had in Munich's butcher shops'.[4]

Some of those who advocated and adhered to a vegetarian way of living wrote eloquently on behalf of the creatures. Ella Wheeler Wilcox put into poetry

> I am the voice of the voiceless
> Through me the dumb shall speak
> Til' the deaf world's ear shall be made to hear
> The wrongs of the wordless weak.[5]

Another 'voice of the voiceless' was Victor Hugo, one-time president of the French Anti-Vivisection Society, who wrote, 'I am certain that when Jesus said, "Do not do to others what you would not wish them to do to you", in his mind the word "others" was immense; "others" surpassed humanity and embraced the universe.'[6] Da Vinci prophesied that 'the time will come when men will look upon the murder of animals as they look upon the murder of men.'[7] Henry David Thoreau echoed the sentiment with, 'I have no doubt that it is part of the destiny of the human race, in its gradual improvement, to leave off eating animals as surely as the savage tribes have left off eating each other.'[8] Tolstoy called the use of animal food 'plainly immoral . . . called forth only by greed'[9]; to Voltaire, it was 'fratricide'[10]; and Shelley, eschewing the universal penchant for euphemism, wrote: 'It is only by softening and disguising dead flesh by culinary preparation that it is rendered susceptible of mastication or digestion, and that the sight of its bloody juices and raw horror does not excite loathing and disgust.'[11]

Some of these luminaires may have been particularly interested in animals, but it would seem more likely that they perceived the 'indivisibility of violence', a phrase coined by English vegan author and publisher, Jon Wynne-Tyson.[12] 'There is not only an indivisibility of violence and cruelty,' he explained to me, 'but an indivisibility of rights. One can't compartmentalize: to be a vegetarian or anti-vivisectionist is not enough in itself; one has to see the whole picture, the holistic man.' This broader view is one element which separates the vegan from the so-called 'animal lover'. Said Wynne-Tyson,

In England particularly there is and always has been a very sentimental element whose professed love of animals is a form of self-love. Fondness of their dogs and cats is, in a strange sort of way, like loving a race horse until it breaks a leg. It's depending upon an animal for pleasure and calling that love.

These 'pet people' are exhibiting a 'humanistic attitude' towards animals, according to a three-year study sponsored by the Fish and Wildlife Service of the United States Department of the Interior. The research conducted by Dr Stephen Kellert and his colleagues was 'to provide objective data on basic attitudes towards animals and to correlate these . . . with socio-economic variables.[13] The humanistic attitude is basically characterized by exceptional personal attachment to animals, usually pets. The eight other attitudes isolated by the researchers were:

1. Naturalistic, with its attraction to wildlife and the outdoors;

2. Ecologistic, more intellectual and detached but also oriented toward wildlife and nature;

3. Scientistic, regarding animals largely as physical objects for study;

4. Aesthetic, also emotionally detached but interested in the symbolic properties or beauty of animals;

5. Utilitarian, in which animals are valued for their material benefit to humans (practical or profitable qualities);

6. Dominionistic, seeing animals as providing opportunities for dominance and control;

7. Negativistic, with its earmarks of indifference, dislike, fear, superstition and general desire to avoid animals; and

8. Moralistic, concern for both wild and domesticated animals coming from an ethical view opposing exploitation, harming or killing animals, rather than out of affection for individual animals or an interest in preserving species; a kinship between humans and animals is generally discerned by persons holding this attitude.[14]

Vegetarians were the most moralistically oriented of the people studied (vegans were not separated from vegetarians). They were found to oppose

hunting, trapping, predator control . . . and much medical research involving the killing of animals. Additionally, they were one of the few moralistically oriented groups which were not also strongly humanistic, embodying a general philosophical concern for animal welfare divorced from any personal affection for animals.[15]

This is not to say that the humanistic attitude and love for pets are entirely absent among vegans. Those who do share their homes with non-humans have generally not sought them out, but have taken in strays that have come to them. Because the traditional pets, cats and dogs, are natural carnivores, the feeding issue must be dealt with. Some vegans feed their animals meat and/or fish since they would be predators if undomesticated. Others might counter this with the question one put to me: 'Do you want the karma of killing a cow to feed a cat?' (I evidently do because I have no plans to take pressure cooker in hand in an attempt to interest my three felines in chick-peas with yeast extract.[16])

There are vegans who have turned their properties into wildlife preserves, such as the 'Unexpected Wildlife Refuge' of Hope and Cavit Buyukmihci in Pennsylvania, and Ruth Howard's 'Sanctuary' in rural Devonshire, but most of the vegans I have contacted, as the Fish and Wildlife Service study might have predicted, are not in direct daily contact with animals to any extraordinary degree. To 'live and let live' is sufficient. Where that simple slogan puts vegans and ethical vegetarians at odds with the rest of society – even with that element sharing the moralistic attitude toward most of the furred and feathered[17] – is regarding human dealings with so-called food animals.

6.

The Vegan Stand

The basic premise of vegetarianism is that humans have no business killing sentient beings for food. The person who argues, 'What if I were stranded on a desert island?' or 'What if I were an Eskimo?' is invariably nowhere near an abandoned isle or an arctic igloo. It has, of course, been contended that animals are not sentient; one who did so was Rene Déscartes, who believed animals to be *automata*, machines, thoughtless and not conscious, lacking a mind or soul, interchangeable concepts in Cartesian philosophy. In his thought, animals may act as if they are feeling pain, but such behaviour is attributable to mere physical laws because, said Déscartes, animals' bodies are part of the material world, the whole of which may be explained via physics. Besides, animals cannot speak and that clearly indicated to him that they could not have consciousness.[1] Although few today would concur with the seventeenth-century French philosopher on this, we often take instead a somewhat snobbish position on just which animals' pain is of consequence. '[That] animals are sentient, can feel pain and pleasure, and have interests and desires which they seek to satisfy . . . we readily admit when speaking of our pets, but tend to forget when eating a bit of an anonymous pig or cow.'[2]

If eating the flesh of that pig or cow were truly necessary for human survival, vegetarians would be either martyrs or fools. On the contrary, however, a well-planned vegetarian diet is conducive to health, strength and longevity. This should not be surprising since, from a physiological perspective, man is generally accepted as being a frugivorous animal like the anthropoid apes. True, Jane Goodall verified that 'Chimps are omnivorous, given the opportunity,'[3] but it is the gorilla, not the chimpanzee, to which man is structurally most akin, and 'Gorillas are strict vegetarians . . . eating chiefly tree ferns and vines[4] . . . various grasses, herbs . . . hedges and shrubs.'[5] Convincing comparative anatomical evidence for a plant-based human diet exists in man's dentition, hand and nail formation, digestive secretions and length of the intestinal canal when these are contrasted with corresponding character-istics of other species.

To further support their position, vegetarians would cite health hazards associated with eating meat (see Chapter 10), land use priorities (see Chapter 7), the high cost of flesh foods, and feedlot and slaughterhouse pollution. Nevertheless, the central concern for the ethical vegetarian is the creature destined to become an entrée. The three areas of potential suffering for that animal are in (1) rearing, (2) transport, and (3) slaughter. 'Humane slaughter' is a relative term that more outspoken vegetarians might juxtapose with 'humane murder' or 'humane rape'. Not the drowsy euthanasia it has been pictured, it means rather that animals are given a high-voltage electric shock or stunned mechanically with a spike penetrating the skull and brain, or a knockout blow to the head that does not penetrate the skull, prior to actual killing. In the USA, use of stunning implements has since 1961 been required of companies that do business with the Federal Government, but smaller, local slaughterhouses can still use antiquated methods: the shackle and hoist, pole-axe or rifle. Stunning has not been routinely utilized in the killing of poultry.[6]

Being transported by rail or lorry to the regional stockyards or directly to the abattoir may involve long confinement in crowded conditions without adequate ventilation, food or water, and in extremes of temperature. Once in the holding pens, animals are often encouraged to move faster with cattle prods capable of producing first degree burns.[7]

Even when aware of these conditions, most people believe them to be only short, final events in otherwise pleasant lives. Whereas the vegetarian could say that he is saving the lives of the 11 cattle, 1 calf, 3 sheep, 23 pigs, 45 turkeys, and 1,097 chickens[8] he would have eaten during a seventy-year lifespan as a 'normal' person, the omnivore could claim that it was his demand for meat that caused those animals to have lived at all. In former times, that may have been a valid position, despite even traditional practices such as de-horning, branding and castration.[9] Since agriculture has largely become agri-business, though, the 'short, happy life is better than no life' theory has lost its credibility. Intensive farming, alluded to earlier, comprises the five essentials of 'rapid turnover, high-density stocking, a high degree of mechanization, a low labour requirement, and efficient conversion of food into saleable products.'[10] These 'controlled environment' systems vary in degree of mechanization from open-air feedlots for pre-market fattening of cattle and pigs (feed is delivered by truck or conveyors and wastes are drained off into holding ponds) to 'total confinement' systems in which

poultry, pigs or calves never see the light of day until they are taken to the slaughterhouse . . . For three months at a stretch, pregnant sows are confined to stalls scarcely larger than their bodies. To reduce stress and activity, totally confined animals are kept in darkness except at feeding time . . .

The new ways are solidly established. About 95 per cent of egg laying hens, virtually all . . . turkeys and half or more of beef cattle, dairy cows and pigs are maintained in some type of factory system.[11]

Although factory farming has increased animal suffering tremendously and therefore fuels the vegetarian argument, it must be remembered that vegetarianism existed well before the mass-meat innovations. Its adherents eschew not just 'farmed' flesh foods but also those obtained by hunting or fishing. Some people who eat fish call themselves vegetarians ('pesco-vegetarian' is the actual term), but this is technically a misnomer. Although some animal rights champions hold that the nervous system of a *shell*fish is primitive enough that eating shrimp or clams is more ethical than consuming cow's milk or battery eggs, the basic vegetarian stand on eating marine animals is that analogized here by Brigid Brophy:

Were it announced tomorrow that anyone who fancied it might, without risk of recriminations, stand at a fourth-story window, dangle out of it a length of string with a meal (labelled 'Free') on the end, wait till a chance passer-by took a bite and then, having entangled his cheek or gullet on the hook hidden in the food, haul him up to the fourth floor and there batter him to death with a knobkerrie, I do not think there would be many takers . . . Yet sane adults do the equivalent to fish every day.[12]

Shooting, too, is regarded as a premeditated act of cruelty, separating animal families and causing a death seldom quick and free from pain. Just as they find no 'charm' in a fox hunt, vegetarians do not see the 'sport' in pitting a creature against a man armed with a rifle, decoys, binoculars, lures and a two-way radio. They denounce the theory that without killing them the animals of the forest would overpopulate and starve: examples of places where shooting has been halted and the animals adjusted without incident are on file at nearly every wildlife protection organization.[13]

Up to this point, vegetarians and vegans are of one mind. The split occurs in the vegan's seeing the entire animal food and products network as a single entity:

True, cowhide is only a by-product of hamburger, but if cows were killed for their skins, would their flesh be any more morally edible so long as you did not wear leather?

And what about the veal floating invisibly inside every glass of milk . . . There can be no quart of milk where there is no cutlet of veal. If your lips are white with milk, it is because someone else's are red with blood.[14]

The vegan is acutely aware that when most people stop eating meat, they increase their egg and cheese consumption markedly 'which means that any relief of suffering for the animals exists more in hope than in fact.'[15] I was personally a prime example of this: it was after becoming a vegetarian, not as a meat-eater, that I could go into ecstasy over a Cheddar omelette. I probably know every eatery in Chicago that serves fluffy omelettes. I even devised a system for protecting myself from the flat variety: a restaurant with linen napkins is sure to make fluffy omelettes; with paper napkins, you take your chances.

In any case, I presumed, as do most of the city-bred, that the cheese for my omelette came indirectly from a creature endowed by nature with extraordinary abilities for milk manufacturing. It never occurred to me that the cow, like any mammalian female, produces milk for her young and must therefore periodically give birth to keep in lactation. I shared with other urbanities the naïve notion that only surplus milk is taken after calves have nursed, but today almost no dairy cow is permitted to suckle her calf more than three days, if that long. According to the 1965 report of the Brambell Committee, a British governmental commission which conducted extensive research into animal treatment in the UK, 'Separating the calf from the mother shortly after birth undoubtedly inflicts anguish on both. Cattle are highly intelligent, and attachment between the calf and the mother is particularly strong.'[16]

A calf may go for almost immediate slaughter as veal, and the rennet from the stomach of one newly born is used in the processing of most commercial cheeses, rendering the product unsuitable for even lacto-vegetarian use in the strictest sense. (Some companies do produce rennetless cheeses which are cultured with vegetable coagulants; these usually have to be purchased at health food shops and are more expensive than the mass-marketed brands.) Those slaughtered early have a more fortunate fate than the calves who go on to white veal units where their fourteen-week lives are spent confined to wooden crates or stalls 1 foot 10 inches wide and 4 feet 6 inches long.[17] They are fed a liquid diet deficient in iron and certain vitamins to promote the desirable paleness of flesh. Lack of roughage induces them to nibble at their crates and hair, and no bedding is provided lest they eat it. (In deference to non-vegetarians concerned about this situation, many have boycotted veal; vegans applaud their efforts but urge them to go further.) A few male calves may be reared for breeding (see Chapter 4) and those females deemed suitable for dairying are fed milk substitutes to encourage precocious development so that at 18-24 months the cycle of continuous pregnancies may begin. These animals will, of course, eventually reach the butcher's. It is curious to note that life in a beef herd is usually much more enjoyable than that endured by dairy cows and their offspring. The calves of beef cattle are

allowed to suckle . . . and graze in the fields until the time comes for the fattening pens and the slaughterhouse, but the surplus calves from the *dairy* herds are often sent to market when a week old (or less) and bought for rearing in intensive beef units . . . encouraged to overeat and . . . kept closely confined so that the minimum proportion of the food is used up for their bodily functions.[18]

The vegan does not see this state of affairs as inconsequential or even as simply an unfortunate necessity in a less than perfect world. He regards egg production similarly. Probably no creature outside the vivisection laboratories is subject to a more pitiable life at the hands of modern man than is the chicken. Those idyllic barnyard scenes with hens pecking outside a chicken coop and the rooster serving as a colourful alarm clock for anyone within earshot still exist in limited number, but the eggs from those family farms don't put a dent in the number consumers demand. To meet this, severely intensive systems have been devised since cage laying and indoor confinement began their rapid spread.

Originally, one bird per cage was the rule. When production increased slightly with two birds per cage and no decline was noted with three, four were tried and now five fully grown hens in a 20 x 24 inch cage is routine in a mid-sized hen battery like the one I visited near Yorkville, Illinois, USA. The 300,000 leghorns of 'White Hen Farms' produce an average of 100,000 dozen eggs each week for a supermarket chain. The 'house' I was allowed to tour is an older two-deck system (that is, two cages high), although White Hen's more modern units are triple-tier. (Some larger batteries – boasting up to one million hens, sometimes packed as tightly as nine to a standard cage – sport wire hen tenements four and five rows high.) White Hen manager Walt Schultz, a personable businessman, explained that 'Higher densities are being researched – more layers per square foot of building . . . It's the only way to be competitive. We have to increase capacity to be more efficient.' And efficient it is: that particular operation runs with twenty-six full-time and eighteen part-time employees, only eight of whom are actually involved in maintaining the birds.

Chickens for such plants are obtained from primary breeders who cage-rear pullets to laying age. The males are spotted by 'sexers' at hatching. 'Usually they go into the discard box where they are left to die. Sometimes they are returned to the incubator; the heavy door is closed, the fan is shut off, and they suffocate.'[19] At 20 weeks, birds ready to lay are transported to the egg farm where they will spend nine months in production. Feed and water are mechanically conveyed in, and eggs and wastes are similarly carried out. Popular in the US is 'stimu-lighting' from fluorescent bulbs overhead, which provides seventeen hours of artificial daylight believed to stimulate laying. Crowded conditions – with a squeeze of four hens into cages of one square foot reported at the Hainsworth Farm in Mt Morris, New York[20] – mean that the birds cannot spread their wings (even one at a time!) and can scarcely turn around; wire flooring often injures their feet and hens have even 'grown fast to their cages'.[21] Under such stresses, the instinctive social structure and 'pecking order' cannot develop, leading to what the industry calls 'vices', notably featherpecking and cannibalism. The British found the afore-mentioned 'stimulighting' to aggravate this so in England dimming of lights, 'twilighting', is preferred.[22] On both sides of the Atlantic, birds are debeaked at one week and again at three to five months when the beak grows back. This, according to zoologist F. W. Rogers Brambell in the previously quoted Brambell Report,

deprives the bird of . . . its most versatile member . . . between the horn and the bone is a thin layer of highly sensitive soft tissue, resembling the 'quick' of the human nail. The hot knife used in debeaking cuts through this complex of horn, bone and sensitive tissue, causing severe pain.[23]

Every instinct – walking about, scratching the earth, dustbathing, nest-building, mating, being part of a flock, experiencing the outdoors – is thwarted, and it all ends with the slaughterhouse and the soup can. ('Broilers' are not as yet raised this intensively on a large scale since the resultant sores and abscesses would diminish their market value.) Ironically, there are laws in both Great Britain and the United States stating that caged birds and animals be given adequate space for basic functions; in both nations' statutes, however, a loophole exists excluding those kept for food from 'equal rights under the law'.[24]

If free-range eggs were widely available at realistic prices, would those who are currently vegan eat them? Some might, although they would then no longer be vegans, but most would still avoid them for the reasons early vegans did. To eat a fertilized egg is in effect to consume a chicken before it is born ('The ethics are borderline,' I was told) and unfertilized eggs, the products of a bird's sexual cycle, can hardly be regarded as natural food for man. Furthermore, vegans choose not to rear food animals themselves and do not ask others to do this for them. Besides, who would support hens past their prime, cows who could no longer produce milk, or the male chicks and calves routinely killed at an early age if there were no meat industry? This is the question vegans put to vegetarians who, understandably, do not care for the question.

There was at one time a strained relationship between UK vegans and their parent organization, the Vegetarian Society.

'The biggest enemy to the development of a plant milk company was the vegetarian who went to one degree but no further,' according to Arthur Ling, director of Plamil, the vegetable milk corporation vegans pioneered. 'Originally, vegetarians didn't want to know about veganism but many have now become vegans. The staunch vegetarian's logic was that they'd only turn the orthodox into vegetarians if they didn't become "fanatic" themselves.' There are still staunch vegetarians but feelings between the two English societies are warm now – the Vegetarian Society is, after all, sponsoring publication of this book – and most of the serious ethical vegetarians I know think of themselves as not being vegan *yet*.

In the United States, the North American Vegetarian Society was nurtured for its first six years by the previously established American Vegan Society which shared its staff, headquarters and resources in hopes of launching a viable, unified vegetarian organization there. Vegans, of course, are usually vegetarian first, so expansion of the latter can only aid the former. Understanding and tolerant for the most part, the vegans I interviewed were not antagonistic toward non-vegan vegetarians, although some were impatient with them. A sampling of attitudes ran:

'They are not fully aware of the meaning of animal exploitation' . . . 'They mean well but have more to learn, as do we all' . . . 'They are hypocritical but at least are making an effort in a positive direction' . . . 'The move to higher ethics is usually gradual' . . . I used to think of veganism as extreme, too, but now I see it as true vegetarianism' . . . 'Sometimes I feel they're hypocritical dilletantes, particularly since they're better informed than the average consumer' . . . 'They are not thinking things through to their logical conclusion; they do not themselves kill but depend on others who do' . . . 'Veganism presents great difficulties to some people and I understand these difficulties' . . . 'I feel people grow at their own rate and I love them at whatever stage they are.'

When the late Jack Sanderson, former president of the Vegan Society, addressed a vegetarian group, be began by congratulating those assembled for the step they had taken on behalf of animals and humankind. The benefit to fellow humans is potentially dramatic and that humanitarian reasoning is currently most persuasive.

7.

Hunger, Ecology, Peace

Most vegans would not be likely to argue with the idea that there is a sort of cosmic unity in which the ultimate ethic of compassion, when followed through fully, benefits all concerned. In adopting a vegan diet, for example, one is helping the animal kingdom, oneself (from the personal health perspective) and, indirectly but importantly, our many hungry human brethren, by freeing up food now used as livestock feed for direct consumption by people who are – right now, this minute – in dire need.

This is not to imply that veganism, even on a large scale, is the sole answer to this global crisis. The picture is as complex as it is tragic and certainly massive social and political changes must take place if we are to avert a rice bowl Armageddon, precursors of which are painfully apparent today in much of the Third World. 'The most important factor contributing to the world food crisis is an unequal distribution of control over agricultural resources . . . that can hardly be solved by mass vegetarian conversions.'[1] However, the inadequate return for land use on an animal diet is such that Addeke H. Boerma, former Director-General of the Food and Agriculture Organization (FAO) of the United Nations has said, '. . . if we are to bring about a real improvement in the diet of the neediest, we must aim at a greater intake of vegetable protein.'[2]

In 1971, the first edition of the book *Diet for a Small Planet* created a minor revolution in the outlook of many Westerners on agricultural methods, the famine and malnourishment ever present throughout much of the world, and on meeting protein needs without subscribing to what author Frances Moore Lappé called 'the great American steak religion'.[3] It is thanks in large part to her book that probably everyone today has at least one friend who 'doesn't eat red meat'. Although not suggesting veganism – dairy products and some fish are included in *Small Planet*'s recipes – Lappé presented to the lay public for the first time the facts of the gross inefficiency of meat as a source of nutriment. She pointed to the enormous quantities of grain and soya consumed by animals to produce a minimal return for human consumption, and refers to these animals as 'protein factories in reverse'. Three pounds of grain and soya must be fed to the chicken for a one-pound return in scrambled eggs or Kentucky fried, four pounds to one for turkey, six to one for pork, and sixteen to one for beef.[4] In terms of protein conversion efficiencies, steers return in annual crude protein yield only 6 per cent of the protein consumed, lamb 9 per cent, pigs 15 per cent, broilers (and eggs) 31 per cent, and milk 27 per cent to 38 per cent.[5]

Dairy products are generally regarded as the superior animal food economically with one pound of grain going to produce one pint of milk,[6] but 'Even the most efficient livestock provide in their products no more than a small fraction of the nutrients they consume.'[7] The FAO estimates that 1-1½ billion people are either hungry or malnourished, and that 500 million of these scarcely have enough food to stay alive.[8] Even so, we continue to devote four-fifths of the planet's agricultural land to the feeding of animals, and only the remaining fifth for feeding human beings directly.[9]

Vegans see two population explosions: that of people in the developing nations, and that of livestock in North America, Western Europe, Australia, and the USSR. These animals, bred by and for man, are in competition with him for vital resources such as water (a vegan diet requires a total industrial, agricultural and domestic consumption of 300 gallons of water per day, a mixed animal and vegetable diet 2,500 gallons[10]) and energy. Ten calories of energy are needed to produce a calorie of feedlot beef, 3 for a calorie of factory-farmed eggs, while for soya beans the energy expenditure is 0.50 and for intensively grown rice, 0.15.[11] The 'impending scarcity of resources . . . would be greatly relieved if less land were used to feed domestic animals . . . The trends in meat consumption and energy are on a collision course.'[12]

As in the animal welfare issues surrounding the consumption of meat, eggs and dairy foods, vegans believe that they have looked at the situation rationally and are acting in the sanest manner possible. True, milk production is more efficient than beef, but without beef, where would all this 'more efficient' milk come from?

Our present violent predatory way of living menaces the health of the whole environment . . . Much publicity has been given lately to the waste of grain in meat production: little has been said of the high protein food, much of it grown in developing countries, that goes to keep cows in milk all the year round.[13]

This is not to imply that vegans do not realize that every move in the right direction is helpful. In theory at least, 'If the average US citizen were to reduce his consumption of beef, pork, and poultry by 10 per cent . . . 12 million tons or more of grain would become available for purposes other than livestock production.'[14] Veganism simply takes a good thing further: there is today approximately one acre of arable land for every man, woman and child on earth;[15] to feed someone on a conventional mixed diet requires 2-3½ acres;[16] a lacto-ovo-vegetarian requires that precious one acre, but a vegan can be sustained in health using only one-fifth of an acre.[17] Because the birth rate of the poor majority is, regretfully, still mushrooming, that difference is critical.

Economic analyst Louis H. Bean has described land use figures in a comprehensible fashion:

An acre of land producing feed for cattle, hogs, poultry or milk can provide a moderately active man with his protein requirements for less than 250 days . . . whereas an acre of dry edible beans will take care of his protein needs for over 1,100 days, split peas 1,785 days, and for edible soybeans over 2,200 days, a ratio of 10 to 1 in favour of soybeans over beef. The productivity of grains lies between these extremes.[18]

If US *feed* crop acreage – more than half the current harvested land total – were to become *food* crop acreage, total food calorie production would be quadrupled.[19] In a vegan world, Britain could, for the first time in her history, become a food exporting nation. This means that, despite the fact that many areas now used for grazing are not suitable for cultivation, there would be ample farmland with sufficient open spaces remaining for recreational parks and wildlife havens.

Some of the land not appropriate for agriculture could accommodate silvaculture, and vegans praise trees highly for their role in the water cycle, helping prevent both flooding and drought, and as windbreaks, soil erosion checks, aids to soil fertility, providers of oxygen, and even, with modern technology, as sources of power and energy. This is all in addition to trees' providing timber and pulp and, in the case of those yielding edible fruits and nuts, maximum food per acre. Trees are also invaluable in desert reclamation, an ironically vegan answer to the meat-connected problem of those deserts, including the Sahara, which were created by man through over-grazing by his domesticated animals. The late Richard St Barbe Baker, the Englishman who instigated the planting of shelter belts to curb the 1930s Dust Bowl in the USA, spearheaded the Sahara reclamation work. He was a vegan and, well into his nineties, was still campaigning for a literal 'greening' of our delicate planetary home. A similar forestry project on a smaller scale has been undertaken in Lesotho in southern Africa as an outreach effort of The Farm, the large Tennessee vegan commune alluded to in Chapter 3 (see also Appendix F).

On a more grassroots level, proving the point of vegan economics personally are Harold and Jenny Bland who live with their young son and daughter on two and a half acres some twenty-five miles from London. They have an exemplary garden and twenty fruit trees, so grocery shopping is only for grains and, until the trees mature, nuts, a concentrated source of protein and fats for vegans. They have planted 400 non-bearing trees during the past year as they look forward to the time, some fifteen years hence, when they will be self-sufficient in fuel. As it is, they use wood rejected by others for the wood-burning stove Mr Bland built from scrap metal. He also constructed the solar oven in which they bake bread and the windmill that provides some of the lighting for the house, although it was developed primarily for scientific purposes and eventual commercial sales. The idea of not wasting is extremely important to them: they buy nothing packaged if it can be avoided and give the dustman only one large bag every nine months; juice is made from windfall apples and extra hot water from the kettle is kept warm in thermos jugs.

More prototypical, perhaps, than typical of vegans, the Blands represent the simple life lived profitably and pleasantly. 'Veganism', says Harold Bland, 'is not an end. It simplifies our lives and enables us to live in the community.' In doing that, he teaches physics and she maths at Stevenage College; they bicycle to work. Part of the 15,000 or so miles that are put on their car each year is from her transporting handicapped people for errands and recreational events. As a family, they enjoy cycle-camping and socializing with friends nearby, most of whom live conventionally. 'People think that living our way would be difficult but once they see it isn't, some will change.'

Of course, there are vegans who live in cities and vegans who generate enough rubbish that the sanitation department wouldn't suspect anything unusual, but on the whole there is an ecological awareness among them. I did not meet one, for example, who favours nuclear power. They are genuinely concerned that non-leather belts, shoes and bags are often plastic, a petroleum derivative and source of pollution. Many conscientiously choose canvas whenever possible; some consider the entire shoe problem a 'difficult ethical decision' but nearly all feel that it is better to go with plastic than to use a slaughterhouse product, especially considering that the abattoir, too, is an infamous polluter. Longtime vegans have seen products created to meet their needs and are confident that when the demand is sufficient, an ecologically sound pseudo-leather will be provided. Meanwhile, vegans live simpler lives than most people and therefore use less plastic overall.

Those who garden – and virtually all try to grow something if they have any space at all – attempt to do so using natural compost methods, and many go beyond organic to veganic gardening, employing no animal manure, bone meal, dried blood fertilizer, etc.[20] Although they live from plant products, they are opposed to wanton destruction even of these and are sensitive to taking from the earth only as much as they need and returning to it all they can. On the issue of killing plants, the composite answer is that since one cannot survive by depending on rays from the sun, one does, by eating plant matter, live destroying the lowest form of life possible at this point. ('If you don't think there is a difference in plant and animal life,' I once heard an Indian vegetarian say, 'why do you take your dog for a walk instead of a cabbage?')

Some plants do not die when harvested, such as fruits and those vegetables that are botanically fruits – cucumber, peppers and the like – and others do not ripen until their life cycle is virtually completed. Although most probably feel that plants do have some sort of consciousness, several pointed out

to me that plants are not likely to feel pain as such since they
have evolved no means of escaping potentially painful stimuli
as have animals and fish. Moreover, vegans point out that they
are not responsible for all the vegetation consumed by animals
they might otherwise have eaten and thus they kill far fewer
plants in the final analysis than do omnivores.

Ecological and social issues are of pressing importance to
vegans and they often combine the two. To the question,
'What do you feel is the greatest world problem?' answers fell
into roughly two categories: one was philosophical, dealing
with man's greed and lack of compassion; the other was
concrete and focused on issues dealt with in this chapter.
Sample replies were:

'Famine resulting from over-population' . . . 'Poverty and starvation,
caused by politicians against the interests of the great populations'
. . . 'The difference in the have and have not peoples' . . . 'Nuclear
weapons and over-population; both endanger all life on our planet'
. . . 'Hunger and drought, mostly caused by over-grazing of animals
and destruction of tree cover causing deserts and poor soil . . . also
nuclear power and pollution from pesticides' . . . 'Hunger; famine;
lack of interesting, safe work; pollution of the environment' . . .
'Overcrowding' . . . 'Shortage of resources' . . . 'War and starvation,
caused by greed.'

According to Professor Henry Baily Stevens, vegan author of
Recovery of Culture, 'The very word for "war" in the Aryan
tongue meant literally "desire for more cows".'[21] Pacifist
Stevens was outspoken in connecting war and butchery: 'The
same brutality appears in stockyard and battlefield. Afterward,
there has been the same reluctance to face the horror of the
means and the emptiness of the ends, the same ability to gloss
and excuse, even to dress vice in the clothes of virtue.'[22] There
are more pacifists to be found among vegans than in the
population at large to be sure. There are among them those
who feel that fighting in time of war can do the greatest good
for the greatest number, but I did not personally meet any who
expressed such a view to me. The closest anyone I contacted
came to that was one woman who said that she opposes
aggression but believes in self-defence and a man who spoke
of war as a 'last resort and very bad for nature'. When asked
how they felt about war, most gave such answers as:

'Killing people as mere representatives of nations is foolish and immoral' . . . 'It is wasteful, destructive, evil and unnecessary' . . . 'If you're vegan, you've got to be a pacifist, haven't you? If you don't kill animals, you don't want to kill people, do you?' . . . 'War creates more problems than it may solve' . . . 'A great social evil' . . . 'An obscenity' . . . 'Sorry state of affairs – some people are still carrying over remnants from centuries past' . . . 'Sad – the karma of our actions can only be eliminated by love, understanding and true non-violence.'

It is certainly easier to recite peaceful prose than to summon the courage to stand by those convictions, yet the vegans I met who had been called upon to take a stand did so valiantly. One English woman became vegan while in gaol for protesting against the arms race, and an American man who was incarcerated for conscientious objection during World War II interested other inmates in his fully non-violent views and became the cook for a popular 'vegetarian table' at the prison. Erstwhile Vegan Society President Sanderson did alternative service during World War II: picking up German fire bombs.

Anti-war sentiments are not unusual, but vegans have a unique vantage point: that 'indivisibility of violence' again. One called war 'inevitable while the philosophy of competition and greed exists', and another brought peace and veganism even closer with: 'A world which lives from killing other animals will eventually kill human animals: the biggest problem in the world is violence and the solution to it is gentleness.'

Can there be a gentle world, a vegan world? People usually think of such a change with genuine alarm. 'Wouldn't the animals overrun the world?' No, those animals are purposely bred. 'Then what would happen to all the cows and ranchers and McDonald's franchises? The answer to all these hypo-thetical panic points is that a vegan world would, at best, be a long time in coming. *If* the incredible 'if' were not so incredible and everyone turned vegan tomorrow, all those freshly compassionate converts would zealously adopt a cow each and labour indefatigably to help locate meaningful work for those freed from what Bernard Shaw called 'man's endless slavery to the animals he exploits'.[23] Stephen Clark addressed himself to the plaint, 'What would happen to civilization?' in *The Moral Status of Animals*: 'To those who speak of the necessity of . . . the supply of food, clothing, perfume, entertainment and medical knowledge which is now at the expense of animal blood and liberty, I only say, "There is none".'[24] In conversation with me, Dr Clark ventured some future projections:

My feeling is that if public feeling continues changing and economically the situation worsens, we're very likely to move toward a low meat diet for most of the population, vegetarianism for many, and a minority of vegans within that. Veganism will grow as we create a new diet. Western tradition is still being proven . . . I don't have hopes of a totally non-violent human species, never killing any creature except under desperate circumstances. The best we can hope for is a world in which non-violence is the approved way.

The best timetable he could give me for this was 'a couple hundred years maybe', but it is starting already. It takes form in earnest every time an individual makes a change in his or her pattern of living that sets into motion the words of the song, 'Let there be peace on earth, and let it begin with me.' One way to do that is by embarking upon the road to veganism.

8.

Making the Break

Some vegans with whom I have talked literally switched overnight: one day they were eating/living conventionally; they
saw some animal cruelty or learned of the circumstances
surrounding a glass of milk, and the next day they were vegan.
In some cases they had never heard the word and did not know
if sustaining life and health on an animal-free diet had ever
been attempted. Most, though, were lacto-ovo-vegetarian first
and dropped products over a period of a year or two; a few
stopped using eggs or dairy before completely eliminating
fish. Non-food commodities were generally phased out over
time, with vegans of two or three years sometimes still wearing
pre-vegan shoes. The important thing, all would agree, is to
make a start. Peter Singer expressed concern in *Animal
Liberation* that when confronted with the vast array of suffering
that exists, one might be too discouraged to attempt *any*
alteration in lifestyle:

'Vegans', then, are right to say that we ought not to use dairy
products. They are living demonstrations of the practicality and
nutritional soundness of a diet that is totally free from the exploitation
of other animals. At the same time, it should be said that, in our
present speciesist world, it is not easy to keep so strictly to what is
morally right. Most people have difficulty enough taking the step to
vegetarianism; if asked to give up milk and cheese at the same time
they could be so alarmed that they end up doing nothing at all. A
reasonable and defensible plan of action is to tackle the worst abuses
first . . . animal flesh and factory farm eggs . . . While someone who
gave up animal flesh and simply replaced it with an increased
amount of cheese would not really be doing very much for animals,
anyone who replaces animal flesh with vegetable protein, while
continuing to eat milk products occasionally, has made a major step
toward the liberation of animals.[1]

Just how to 'tackle those worst abuses' is an individual matter. Frances Moore Lappé suggests starting with one new menu or ingredient a week until one has built up a repertoire of enjoyable new dishes,[2] but for one concerned with immediate animal suffering as well as with world hunger, that process would prove too slow. On the other hand, Jay Dinshah suggests eliminating meat, fish and fowl immediately, then eggs, then dairy, and 'Along with the animal junk, throw out all the white-as-death rice, flour and sugar, and the tinned, preserved processed "foods" . . . fried foods of any type . . . tobacco . . .'[3] These additional 'reform' measures are not taken by all vegans; two young animal activists wrote for *The Vegan*:

To us Veganism is solely about stopping suffering . . . So where do health foods come in, how does the use of brown rather than white flour help animals? . . .

Like most people, we live on a trash diet . . . We have neither the time or the self interest to worry about health foods, and eat nuts only at Xmas [*sic*].[4]

Vegans holding this opinion – they are a minority – believe that adding 'health foods' to an already unconventional diet could discourage potential converts. The 'other side' suggests that it is only through vibrant health and vigour that others can be attracted to their way of life; they also contend that we owe as much kindness to our 'animal' bodies as we do to animals. 'Our first responsibility is to ourselves,' a Londoner in his early thirties told me. 'We deserve the best, not second-best protein. There is a misconception that veganism is first, but *you're* first. To get people to change, you provide the food, provide an alternative; make it the best food they've ever eaten.' He and his friends live up to that: the evening I visited, they served salad, soup made from miso[5], freshly baked wholemeal bread, nut burgers, runner beans, and tofu[6] cheesecake. Moderation and simplicity are set aside when entertaining, even among vegans!

A successful method of switching from non-vegetarian living is to purchase a few good vegan cookbooks and start experimenting with the entrées in them. Meat and fowl could then be eliminated, and battery eggs replaced with the free-range ones from a wholefood shop or direct from an old-style farm. Cheese, even fish, might remain temporarily for dining out and socializing. Vegan cheeses (see Chapter 14, Recipes) would eventually replace dairy cheese at home and various soya and nut milks (commercial or kitchen-blended) could fill the void left by cow's milk. Even with tapering off, though, a leap of faith, 'this is it' moment of decision has to come. Then it is completed.

Scouting out restaurants can take some doing if one expects to eat major meals out: vegetarian or wholefood restaurants are excellent certainly, and so are many ethnic ones – Indian (vegetable curries), Chinese (vegetable chop suey or chow mein), Italian (pasta with tomato or mushroom sauce), Middle Eastern (dishes based on chick peas, tahini and aubergine), but a conscientious vegan checks ahead to be sure that vegetable oil, not lard, is used in the cooking process. In England, 'salad sandwiches' and 'beans on toast' are offered nearly everywhere. In the States, cafeterias are easy; so are salad bars, smorgasbords, and 'good' restaurants which have delicious à la carte vegetables, nice salads, and will provide a special vegan meal on request, as will most airlines. Some vegans are simply abstemious and don't mind an occasional meagre meal; others carry a few nuts, a little dried fruit, or a tiny jar of peanut butter to give meals eaten at unaccommodating places more substance. Most of the vegans I queried go to non-vegetarian restaurants only on occasion: they can eat better at home without supporting meat-oriented businesses.

Accepting the hospitality of non-vegan friends is not avoided, although tact is required in explaining – simply, briefly, and with a light touch – that no animal food is eaten. Comments on this included:

'I just eat the vegetables, grains and fruit, and sometimes bring my own' . . . 'I let them know in advance of my preferences' . . . 'I eat only the vegan parts although I have at times compromised to vegetarian food' . . . 'We inform new friends beforehand of some simple ideas or take along a food gift to help out' . . . 'I take my own pre-cooked meals for re-heating' . . . 'I've sometimes given them a recipe book!' . . . 'It is at times difficult but they know my limits and I do not feel I must question ingredients in breads, cakes and so forth to the point of alienating their interest' . . . 'I just don't eat anything that isn't vegan; I don't make a fuss' . . . 'I try to inform them and invite them to my house first' . . . 'I take them something special to get them interested in vegetarianism' . . . 'I can always find something to eat.'

But just what *do* vegans 'find to eat'? I asked for sample day's menus:

American male, 29 years old, 5'9", 140 lb, vegan 7 years:
> Breakfast: Sunflower seed milk with carob powder[7], grated apple, wheatgerm.
> Lunch: Salad and sandwich, i.e. bean spread on pitta bread.
> Dinner: Salad, steamed green vegetable, macaroni and vegan cheese.

British female, 40 years old, 5'8", 121 lb, vegan 11 years:
> Breakfast: Wholemeal toast with vegan margarine, half grapefruit and apple.
> Lunch: Mixed salad (lettuce, carrot, beetroot, cabbage, bean sprouts, etc.) with crispbread, nuts and raisins.
> Dinner: Baked potato with lentil or nut savoury, rice dish or pulses, salad, fresh fruit.

American female, 26 years old, 5'6", 128 lb, vegan 6 years:
> Breakfast: Compote of bananas, apple sauce, raisins, seeds.
> Lunch: Watermelon 'smoothie' (blender purée with optional additions of nuts, protein powder, other fruit, etc.)
> Dinner: Green salad, carrot salad, millet burgers, steamed spinach.

British male, 36 years old, 6'2", 157 lb, vegan 14 years:
> Breakfast: Muesli[8]
> Lunch: Peanut butter and yeast extract[9] sandwiches, salad.
> Dinner: Cooked vegetables, bean stew, fruit cake.

American female, 29 years old, 5'5", 110 lb, vegan 2 years:
> Breakfast: Cereal,[10] toast, juice.
> Lunch: Peanut butter, crackers, herbal tea.
> Dinner: Stir-fried vegetables with tofu over brown rice, juice.

British female, 72 years old, 5'0", 108 lb, vegan 23 years:
> Breakfast: Muesli with vegetable milk or fruit juice, toast with vegan margarine and yeast extract.
> Lunch: Large green salad with fresh fruit and dates, baked potato or bread with vegan cheese.
> Dinner: Lightly cooked vegetables with soya 'steak' or bean pie.

American male, 67 years old, 5'7", 150 lb, vegan 38 years:
  Breakfast: Orange juice, 2 slices wholemeal bread, 2 bananas.
  Lunch: Raw salad, 2 or 3 cooked vegetables.
  Dinner: Large raw salad, split pea soup, baked potato, 2
                cooked vegetables.

British female, 19 years old, 5'5", 105 lb, vegan 3 years:
  Breakfast: Porridge, fruit, coffee.
  Lunch: Nuts, fresh and dried fruit.
  Dinner: Cooked vegetables, grains, beans.

Vegan foods needn't be so odd that they require footnotes. Dr Julian Whitaker, a California heart specialist who puts all his patients on a vegan regimen, insisted in my interview with him that it is entirely possible to nourish oneself adequately and interestingly with foods available at any large supermarket. 'My patients are Middle American all the way; they don't shop at health food stores.' Still, as the samples indicated, most vegans find that certain unusual foods both add variety to their meals and enhance total nutrition. Although they tend to look for fresh food virtually 'as it comes' from orchard, field or garden, when processed items are purchased, American vegans read labels to be certain there is no animal shortening, dairy whey, egg albumen, etc., present. British labelling regulations are not as specific as those required in the USA ('edible oil', to give a particularly confounding example, can mean almost anything, even whale oil) so the Vegan Society's commodities investigator corresponds with individual companies to keep a continually updated list of prepared items suitable for members' use.

That is only the gustatory side of veganism, though. What about all those other articles and erstwhile amusements vegans choose to shun? Few people come to veganism while still hunters or fishermen, and not many would be likely to have fur coats in their closets. Practically anyone's closet, however, is apt to house garments of leather, silk and wool, and non-vegan toiletries live in nearly everybody's medicine cabinet – right next to the non-vegan medicines.[11] Leather has been dealt with earlier: vegans wear shoes and belts of canvas, cloth, straw, cork, rubber and manmade materials. Silk, for those who miss it, is substituted with synthetic fabrics because 'Genuine silk is almost universally obtained by first roasting or boiling the silkworm to death (a process euphemistically known as "stifling") while the little creature is still in its cocoon.'[12]

Wool, like honey, is slightly controversial because it can obviously be taken without killing the animal and we were taught from childhood that sheep must be relieved of their heavy 'coats' for their own comfort. Most vegans would reply that the wool and mutton industries are rather one industry, and that much of the wool used (in the USA in any case) is in fact 'pulled wool', taken from the sheep at the time of slaughter.[13] That domesticated sheep have 'too much wool' is, say vegans, due to selective breeding by profit-motivated humans. Hundreds of thousands of mature sheep die yearly of cold soon after shearing and in Australia alone a 10 per cent loss of lambs within a few days after birth, due largely to flock size and inadequate stockmen, is considered 'unavoidable'.

On an educational radio programme for children, a sheep farmer explained that every shearer has a blood-stauncher standing by whose duty it is to dab tar on the cuts . . .

Of course, it is just possible that the wool for that attractive pullover you were planning to buy came from sheep which had never been chilled, branded, bought, jostled and sold in a market-place like an old saucepan . . . but the odds are against it.[14]

With those 'odds', vegans opt for cotton and synthetic fibres for coats, suits, sweaters, carpeting and rugs. The Beauty Without Cruelty charity has long sought out fashions of non-animal origin (fake fur coats in particular) and informs members and enquirers of how to obtain these. *The Vegan* also offers suggestions in each issue, the facts compiled by the commodities investigator who writes to companies one at a time. Otherwise, shopping includes making a game of reading content tags and, for older vegans, gratitude that it is much easier now than in the early days.

Superior American food labelling is balanced by Britain's more liberal cosmetic testing laws. In the USA, virtually every cosmetic ingredient other than those accepted as 'food grade' has been tested on laboratory animals. This is true in England as well but to a lesser extent so that companies which so choose may test their products on human volunteers who wear the make-up or use the cleanser for an extended period of time and monitor results. Referring to such testing of the Beauty Without Cruelty line,

It is not a heroic act on their part to use a product that would not harm human or animal and that can only beautify and benefit. We believe that products of nature's bounty have an affinity with the human organism and that their assimilation creates balance which results in beauty of skin texture, tissue firmness, etc.[15]

The testing on animals, though, is not an innocent matter of nose-powdering or paw-polishing, although even such fairy tale possibilities would interfere with a creature's right to a natural, dignified life. The tests employed include the Draize rabbit blinding test (see Chapter 1, note 5) under fire presently from combined animal welfare groups in the USA, and the LD-50 test. In that, the beauty product (or drug, pesticide, floor polish, food additive, etc.) is force-fed or injected in progressively higher dosages into rats, dogs, monkeys and/or representatives of other species; the lethal dosage is determined as that which brings the total number dead up to fifty per cent. The remaining animals are killed. In the skin irritancy test, creams, make-up, tanning preparations and so forth are applied to two sections of skin on animals restrained in stocks: one section is simply shaved, while the other is scraped off or peeled away exposing sensitive tissue beneath; the damage caused is noted in 'scoring' the substance.[16]

In addition to their having undergone animal testing, cosmetics and toiletries probably include slaughter ingredients – anything from beef fat in soap (soap factories are often located conveniently close to abattoirs) to hormonal extracts in so-called nourishing creams. These hormones are derived from the urine of pregnant horses, kept on isolated PMU (Pregnant Mare Urine) farms, confined in special harnesses, allowed no exercise, and given an unnatural diet to encourage urine production.[17] To avoid supporting what seem to vegans to be horror story enterprises, they shop for different products: pure Castile soaps, those formulated for kosher Jewish use, or others specially created without animal ingredients. (Faith, Creighton, Tom's, Tiki, and Weleda manufacture vegan bar soap, and the Mellow Food Company makes a nice liquid one.) For laundry, a vegan might simply grate bar soap and use it with washing soda, or seek out a suitable commercial product such as Janco Biodegradable Liquid Soap which can also be used for washing up, cleaning surfaces, and even as bubble bath. Jane Howard Ltd (Appendix H) puts out a complete range of vegan complexion care items, and women who use make-up and fragrance can turn to Beauty Without Cruelty Ltd (see Appendix G) or other firms dedicated to producing cruelty-free cosmetics. Both the soap and the beauty products companies offer a wide range of hair care items.

Hairbrushes, then, would have nylon or plastic bristles instead of boar; pillows would be foam, not feather; sleeping bags polyester, not down. Handbags might be cotton or canvas; shoes are anything but leather or suede. Cotton, linen, and synthetic fabrics are used in clothing and furnishings. Shopping can be seen as an adventure and a mission.

And shopping for food is a real delight, resulting in a most special place, a vegan kitchen. During this writing, I have tried to make mine an exemplary one, so I offer it for a brief tour: there are containers filled with grains – brown rice, oats, pot barley, wholewheat berries, millet, and wholegrain pastas – and pulses: lentils, butter beans, chick peas, akuki beans, pinto beans, split peas, and soya beans. Alfalfa, chick pea and mung bean sprouts grow in jars on the countertop. In the refrigerator are flours (wheat, rye, soya, barley, maize meal), raw nuts (almonds, hazelnuts, Brazils, peanuts, cashews), seeds (sesame, pumpkin, sunflower), peanut butter, and cold-pressed oil, most of which are purchased at natural food retailers.[18] The bread on hand is usually purchased (there is wholemeal vegan bread to be bought; read the labels), but if I've baked I get both bread and that wonderful aroma throughout my flat. Soft vegan margarines are found in health food shops (Vitaquell and Vitaseig are popular British brands; Tomor, a hard margarine, can be found in health food shops throughout Britain.)

There are some tinned foods on my shelves for hurried evenings: beans, tomatoes, unsweetened fruit. (Dried foods and meals like the vegan line from Direct Foods Ltd are also quick.) Nearly everything else is produce: fresh, frozen and dried fruits, fresh or frozen vegetables, many local and seasonal, and a couple of kinds of juices. There is yeast extract, natural soya sauce ('tamari'), a host of dried herbs, and various vegetable seasonings to perk up the fare. Then there's the cat food. I never claimed to be perfect.

9.
Nutritional Considerations

A balanced diet is as necessary for a vegan as for anyone else but, contrary to popular opinion, it is not *more* necessary: one need neither go for a degree in dietetics nor become a food faddist to be a well-nourished total vegetarian. A simple way to insure adequate nutrition is through an adaptation of the 'Four Food Groups'. For omnivores and lacto-vegetarians, those are: (1) meat and meat alternates, (2) dairy products, (3) fruits and vegetables, and (4) breads and cereals with an obvious overemphasis on animal products. The vegan products are:

1. *Legumes, nuts and seeds* – which may be made into entrées of various types (soups, stews, loaves, patties, rissoles, burgers, croquettes, casseroles, etc.); TVP (textured vegetable protein), the commercial meat analogues, would also fall into this category;

2. *Vegetables* – an amazing array of which may be used raw in handsome salads, or lightly steamed, baked, served with sauces or as part of an entrée; when the dark greens (kale, collards, mustard and turnip greens) are included, one goes far towards filling calcium needs which for others would be met largely by dairy foods;

3. *Fruits* – eaten fresh or dried, out of hand or in salads, *compotes*, or desserts, blended into 'milkless shakes', drunk as juices, or occasionally baked or stewed;

4. *Whole grains* – cooked as cereals, entrée bases or side dishes, sprouted as vegetables (any whole grain, bean or seed may be sprouted), or baked into breads, muffins, pie crusts, biscuits, etc.

By choosing from these groups each day and eating a goodly amount of uncooked food, one is assured of sufficient protein, carbohydrates, fats, fibre, minerals and vitamins for health.

'Where do you get your protein?' is the first question any vegetarian is asked (right before the ones about desert islands and Eskimos). The answer is 'Everywhere!' because every natural food contains protein, although in some the amounts are small. Vegans are pleased to get firsthand protein: that in steak or cheese, they say, is grass and grain protein cycled through the body of an animal. Concentrated vegetable protein sources are legumes or pulses, grains, and nuts, seeds and their butters. A usually unsuspected source of protein is found in the dark greens like cos lettuce and kale. Protein is comprised of amino acids, eight of which are considered 'essential' since they cannot be synthesized within the human body and must therefore be ingested. Vegetable foods were formerly referred to as a 'second-class' source of protein, because few contain all eight 'essential' amino acids in appreciable quantities. This is no longer the consensus: a combination of two vegetable protein sources such as rice and beans, peanut butter on wholemeal bread, or waffle batter containing oats and sunflower seeds, makes

... a case where the whole is greater than the sum of its parts ... this is true because the EAA [essential amino acid] deficiency in one food can be met by the EAA contained in another food ... combinations can increase the protein quality as much as 50 per cent above the average of the items eaten separately.[1]

This is a simplified view of protein complementarity as espoused by Lappé in the original editions of *Diet for a Small Planet*. It need not be complicated (who eats peanut butter without bread?) and later research has shown that the need for combining proteins may have been overemphasized:

At any given time, the body is drawing upon a blood pool of amino acids that contributes many of the amino acids required. Therefore, if one meal were to contain a paucity of one or two of them, this would not compromise the overall body processes. However, [a] large raw vegetable salad with an abundance of green foods and sprouts ... with some ... concentrated food ... nuts or seeds or perhaps some sort of grain, supplies a variety of amino acids that's fully adequate.[2]

Many strong and long-lived people thrive on protein intakes one-quarter that of the average Westerner.

Members of primitive cultures who take in twenty-five grams of protein and one gram of salt a day are lean and physically fit, with virtually no sign of degenerative disease. Americans who eat 110 grams of protein every day are rushing to health food stores for protein powder. What is the symptom of an American adult with a protein deficiency? We don't know; we've never seen any. We're afraid of something and we don't even know what it is.[3]

The American Recommended Daily Allowance for protein has been lowering with time; the current recommendation is 56g for men and 44g for women (pregnant women and nursing mothers require more of all nutrients). The male allowance could be met by 3oz of peanuts, a bowl of split pea soup, two slices of wholemeal toast, and a 10oz glass of soya milk.[4] This is, of course, without even taking into account the protein contained in all the other foods he would eat that day.

Complex carbohydrates are the mainstay of a vegan diet. These carbohydrates – vegetables, fruits and grains – provide energy, contain a wealth of vitamins and minerals, and even those foods generally thought of as starches (grains, for example) are protein sources as well. Health-conscious vegans avoid refined carbohydrates (white flour, white rice, de-germinated maize flour, etc.) and sugars (granulated or powdered sugar, golden treacle and so forth) and products containing them.

Fats in a vegan diet come from nuts, seeds, avocado, any oils used in salad dressings or for cooking, and margarine if taken. These vegetable fats are free from cholesterol (see Chapter 10, 'A Holistic Look at Health and Vegans'). A vegan diet is easily kept low in total fat while at the same time providing adequate amounts of essential fatty acids.

Fibre (bulk, roughage) is the non-nutritive portion of foodstuffs necessary for proper intestinal activity. Vegans did not have to get on the bran bandwagon popular a few years back, because their way of eating affords ample roughage from whole grains, raw fruits and vegetables, nuts and seeds.

A varied vegan diet is rich in necessary minerals. Two of particular importance are iron, required for supplying the blood with oxygen and in red blood cell formation, and calcium which aids in blood-clotting and muscle formation, and is essential for strong teeth and bones. Iron is found abundantly in dried apricots, blackstrap molasses, oats, soya beans, prune juice, sesame seeds, sunflower seeds, wheatgerm, nutritional yeast and many other non-animal foods. Lacto-vegetarians who have had difficulty in maintaining adequate haemoglobin levels due to their high intake of iron-deficient dairy foods often discover that upon becoming vegan, that problem is solved.

Calcium, on the other hand, is a mineral many would-be vegans fear they will miss if they cease to use milk products. It is true that in Western Europe and the USA, we depend upon milk and cheese for calcium, but that does not mean that other common foods do not equal or surpass milk in this element. A 100g edible portion of milk contains 118mg of calcium and that amount of Swiss cheese is indeed rich at 925mg. However, 100g of almonds yields 234mg of calcium, wholemeal bread 118, raw kale 179, sunflower seeds 120, and turnip greens 246 – with a calorie cost of only 15 and a 'trace' of fat, compared with over 300 calories and 9g of fat for the cheese. The American Recommended Daily Allowance for calcium is 800mg, readily attainable on a vegan diet, even though it has been suggested that the figure is unnecessarily high for a vegan since it is based on the needs of 'average' people who consume inordinate amounts of meat. Because meat is high in phosphorus, a necessary element but one which needs to be kept in approximately a one-to-two ratio with calcium, ominvores require more calcium than their vegetarian counterparts.

Nuts, whole grains and legumes provide magnesium, zinc and trace minerals. Iodine comes in sea salt or iodized salt, vegetables grown in areas in which there is a substantial iodine content in the soil, and in edible seaweeds such as kelp and dulse. Sea vegetation, rich in protein and low in fat and calories, is almost a vitamin/mineral supplement in itself; it may be used in granular form as a salty seasoning or as a vegetable in salads and oriental cuisine.

Some seaweeds have even been found to contain vitamin B_{12}, the one known element not believed to be available in plant sources unless they hve been contaminated by the micro-organisms that produce this unique vitamin. B_{12}, or cyanocobalamin, functions in normal cell division and in the production of DNA and RNA. Deficiency can be serious: megaloblastic anaemia and sub-acute combined degeneration of the spinal cord.[5] The amount of B_{12} needed is miniscule – 1-3 micrograms per day – but vital. Probably more clinical studies involving vegans have been done regarding this factor than any other. It has been hypothesized that some vegans may be able to synthesize B_{12} in their intestinal tracts in such a way that it can be utilized by the body. Nevertheless, almost all choose to supplement their diet with a source of B_{12}: the fortified plant milks, yeasts or yeast extracts, or in tablet form (the B_{12} is cultured from moulds so the tablets are non-animal), and possibly by eating tempeh. A fermented soya bean product used like meat, tempeh acquires naturally occurring cyanocobalamin through the fermentation process. The need for care in obtaining this nutrient does not dissuade those vegans who maintain that theirs is the proper diet for our species:

It is an ironical fact that man living in a truly natural state like the animals, uninhibited by civilized man's excessive regard for cleanliness and hygiene, would probably get by. Thus, rhesus monkeys on a fruitarian diet in hygienic captivity sometimes suffer from B_{12} deficiency, though they are healthy in the wild.[6]

The other vitamin some vegans supplement at times (i.e. in winter, during pregnancy, and for children) is vitamin D, needed for proper calcification of bones. It is best obtained by the action of direct sunlight on the skin, but since most people do not get sufficient exposure to the sun during much of the year, milk and butter are fortified with vitamin D. Lacking these, vegans depend on fortified margarine, vitamin drops or tablets (irradiated ergosterol is the non-animal source), or spending more time outdoors.

Because plants are veritable vitamin factories, vegan diets abound in the other known ones, notably:

Vitamin	A few vegan sources
A	Apricots, melon, winter squash, carrots, spinach, cress.
B_1 (Thiamin)	Peanuts, wheatgerm, sunflower seeds, brown rice, nutritional yeast.
B_2 (Riboflavin)	Leafy vegetables, almonds, whole grains, nutritional yeast.

B_3 (Niacin)	Peanut butter, wholemeal bread, lentils, mushrooms.
B_6 (Pyridoxine)	Bananas, cabbage, corn-on-the-cob, oats, split peas, wheat.
C	Citrus fruits, green peppers, tomatoes, potatoes, cabbage, strawberries.
E	Unrefined vegetable oils, wheatgerm, haricot beans, sweet potatoes, turnip greens.
K	Dark green leafy vegetables, alfalfa sprouts, soya bean oil, tomatoes.

Most of the vegans I questioned do not take vitamin or mineral supplements (other than B_{12} as discussed), reasoning that because nutrition is not yet an exact science and myriad elements are likely yet to be isolated, the most sensible dietetic approach is to eat a variety of natural foods which have been subjected to a minimum of processing or preparation. For those who do use vitamins, several companies now market total-vegetarian lines free from fish-liver oil, bone meal, desiccated liver and other glandular extracts, eggshell and oyster shell calcium, and other commonly used ingredients of animal origin.

As a group, vegans are keenly aware of the importance of good nutrition for physical well-being, but they are equally adamant that it is not the paramount concern of life. 'Thinking probably has more to do with health than diet does,' said Serena Coles, an English vegan of forty-five years whose energy level is astonishing. Whether it is their eating, their thinking, or a combination of the two, the people themselves are their lifestyle's best advertisement.

10.
A Holistic Look at Health and Vegans

When vegans and the medical teams that have studied them laud their diet, its benefits seem to come at least as much from what they're not eating as from what they eat:

Consumption of animal fat and meat have been linked conclusively with an elevated incidence of heart disease, stroke, cancer of the colon and breast, liver and kidney disease, depletion of the bone mass, arthritis and a host of other afflictions.[1]

Arteriosclerotic damage is more pronounced in Americans at 30 years of age than in Japanese of 70 who, although they eat fish, consume little or no meat, eggs or dairy produce; the heart disease rate in Japan is one-tenth the US rate[2] although the two nations are equally industrialized. Even so conservative an organ as the *Journal of the American Medical Association* editorialized that a completely vegetarian diet 'could prevent 90 per cent of our thrombo-embolic disease and 97 per cent of our coronary occlusions'.[3]

Animal foods have been indicted as possible precipitators of cancer due both to their fat content and substances added to them in modern production. Among these are: nitrosamines which result as a chemical reaction to sodium nitrate and nitrite used in cured meats; the hydrocarbons from charcoal-broiling; and malonaldehyde, used in rancidity testing and found in meat and appreciable quantities yet negligibly in fruits and vegetables. 'The results', commented Dr Raymond J. Shamberger who researched malonaldehyde, 'are consistent with the observations that vegetarians have lower cancer death rates.'[4] Synthetic hormones, such as the widely publicized DES (diesthylstilbestrol) are boons to the livestock trade in that they encourage rapid growth and weight gain without a corresponding increase in feed, but they have been strongly implicated as carcinogenic. Admittedly, it sometimes seems that everything is a suspected carcinogen, but 'Since 1959, more than twenty countries have banned DES and other growth hormones used in livestock production. Italy and Sweden banned importation of US DES-fed beef.'[5]

Other hygienic objections to meat include the cell decomposition or decaying process known as 'ageing' or 'ripening' and the toxic wastes such as uric acid and bacteria present in flesh foods. To mitigate bacterial contamination, antibiotics are routinely added to animal feeds, resulting in drug residues in meat and milk, and encouraging the growth of antibiotic-resistant bacteria.[6] The phenomenon of 'pain poisoning', the release into an animal's system of adrenaline during times of stress, produces physical changes in the carcass; even an American Meat Institute spokesman confessed in 1971 that 'there are many more implications to pain-poisoning that are yet to be understood.'[7] Meat inspection, also, is not as complete as one would expect: an American agricultural inspector may, for example, have to examine up to 1,100 pig carcasses in a single hour. 'It was also found that if a cancerous tumour, for example, is discovered, the infected animal which nurtured that particular malignancy is passed on for human consumption.'[8] Finally by eating lower on the food chain, vegans escape the heftier concentrations of pesticide residues present in all foods of animal origin.[9]

British clinical investigations into the health of vegans have shown that they are at least *as* healthy as vegetarians and omnivores, that they exhibit lower serum cholesterol levels than either of the other groups, and have a markedly decreased likelihood of developing such 'diseases of civilization' as angina pectoris, arterioslcerosis, ischemic heart disease[10] and certain cancers. 'The vegan diet, when fortified with vitamin B_{12}, is fully adequate. You can't tell vegans from omnivores except that they're slimmer and perhaps smile more.'[11] Epidemiological studies of cultures whose members eat vegan or near-vegan diets underline these conclusions[12] and they have been further confirmed by research on American vegans headed by Dr Mervyn G. Hardinge of the Loma Linda University School of Public Health in California. He and his colleagues found the vegans in their studies to be free of any clinical deficiency symptoms and to weigh on average '12 kg less than the lacto-ovo-vegetarians and the nonvegetarians, who average 8-10 kg above the "ideal" weight.'[13]

Although no solid clinical evidence exists in support of it, the physical benefit most frequently cited by vegans I interviewed was the alleviation of respiratory complaints ranging from frequent colds to bronchitis and chronic asthma, when they stopped drinking milk. 'Nature cure' theorists have long taught that dairy products are 'mucus forming' and practising vegans would appear to bear this out. Curiously, most adults in the world cannot tolerate milk anyway! The enzyme lactase needed for digesting milk sugar, lactose, is lacking in all but a minority of the human population, being present mainly in Caucasians whose cultures have used dairy products for many centuries. So-called 'lactose intolerance' affects, among others, 90 per cent of Thais and Filipinos, 85 per cent of the Japanese, and 70 per cent of American blacks.[14] This comes as no surprise to vegans who have always maintained that milk is a baby food and the milk intended for any infant mammal is that of its own species.[15]

Also reported to me as health plusses resulting from veganism were lower blood-pressure, relief from migraine, eczema and other skin disorders, and from rheumatic distress. Some commented that as vegans they had less of a tendency towards overweight (see 'Slimming on a Vegan Diet' in Part 2), and many spoke of having more energy and stamina. These traits are particularly evident in vegan athletes such as Channel swimmer Jack McClelland, English wrestler Harry Bonnie, and US Marine Corps Captain Alan M. Jones who, on an almost one hundred per cent vegan diet, has broken endurance records with amazing frequency. He holds the world's record for sit-ups (27,000), swam 500 miles on the Snake and Columbia Rivers in the northwestern United States in eleven days, skipped rope 43,000 times in five hours and – one month later – 100,000 times in twenty-three hours.[16] (There are many famous vegetarian athletes – swimmer Murray Rose, body-builder Andreas Cahling, basketball stars Bill Walton and Pete Maravich, and baseball's Pete LaCock and Bill Lee to name a few – but I do not have information on which, if any, of these are total vegetarians, i.e. dietary vegans.)

Some of the people with whom I spoke noted no particular changes in their state of health after becoming vegan, but in none had it deteriorated in any way. Many commented on an improved mental attitude and emotional poise resulting from a more consistently compassionate lifestyle:

'I feel better about myself because I know I'm not hurting animals' . . . 'One benefit is not feeling so greedy in face of world poverty' . . . 'I have better health and better spirits' . . . 'My mind is clearer' . . . 'I feel an inner peace yet there is a need to be much more thoughtful about every action in life.'

One such action is the decision on the sort of practitioner to consult if one should become ill. Animal gelatin, blood and glands are common pharmaceutical ingredients; all drugs and surgical procedures have, of course, been tested on animals in laboratories; and the very process of medical education and the scientific schooling which precedes it are rife with vivisection. No less than Carl Jung as he described his own medical training in *Memories, Dreams, Reflections*, spoke of animal experimentation as 'horrible, barbarous and above all unnecessary'.[17] Vegans would concur, but this does not mean that they resolutely avoid all medical doctors. In fact, some noted MD's of the past and present have practised veganism and supported its aims; one of these was the late Dr Frey Ellis, an eminent British cardiologist who served as president of The Vegan Society. Nevertheless, vegans conscientiously seek to do without drugs when at all possible. Slightly different views on this were expressed in letters to *The Vegan* in 1969. One member wrote:

I feel that in special circumstances vegans should accept drugs . . . Each of us must realize that when one of us dies it is one less to fight against the atrocities which are being committed.[18]

Another responded:

I am sure that the choice must be an individual one . . . Much depends upon our own inner knowledge of the healing possible within our individual cells . . . I was threatened with pneumonia when I refused injections, but I succumbed to anaesthetics when having bones set! . . . What a great need there is for more . . . knowledge of herbal healing which does not leave the side effects that drugs tend to have. Let us try to work with nature – even if we have unnatural accidents![19]

Vegans are generally open to herbalism and other forms of natural therapeutics, represented by naprapathy and massage, naturopathy, chiropractic, homoeopathy, osteopathy (in Britain, osteopathy remains a drugless healing profession, but in the USA today it is virtually indistinguishable from allopathy), and Natural Hygiene, which considers itself a way of living rather than a healing system. Practitioners in these fields fit the description attributed to Thomas Edison that 'The doctor of the future will give no medicine, but will interest his patients in the care of the human frame, in diet, and in the cause and prevention of disease.'[20] Modalities some of them would employ may be structural (spinal adjustment, body manipulation, postural alignment, exercise, physical therapy), chemical (alterations in eating habits, special cleansing diets and/or fasting, herbs, nutritional supplementation), or environmental (therapeutic baths, hot and cold applications, extra rest or increased exposure to fresh air and sunshine). Some of these healing arts practitioners might use acupuncture and others yogic principles, guided relaxation, and meditation; and some vegans do look to various forms of mental or spiritual healing. On the whole, they are essentially healthy without belabouring the issue.

Their general outlook on life is refreshingly positive. In spite of the cruelty and ugliness of which they are so acutely aware, most seem too involved in changing things to bemoan their present state. They are not Pollyanna types nor, as indicated early on, ripe for canonization: at times, a vegan is apt to gossip or criticize, to be as rude or resentful or angry as anybody else. Veganism neither requires nor implies any change in character or demeanour, although some believe that those changes do take place. While many would emphasize they 'have not forsworn flesh because I think "the flesh" is evil or because I feel contaminated by its passing my lips',[21] others would more nearly agree with Tolstoy: 'If a man's aspirations toward a righteous life are serious . . . his first act of abstinence is from animal food.'[22] It is, then, paradoxical: is it a matter of 'you are what you eat' or that one eats, and lives, in a certain way because of the traits and inclinations that comprise his very selfhood? Speaking from the former perspective was the young Englishman who believes

Anybody, everybody could come to veganism: your gentleness is related to the food you eat. In Oriental diagnosis, meat eaters have liver marks; the liver is related to anger. The coordination of your organs makes your personality. Food isn't everything but it's something a person can change. Vegans aren't 'special people'.

Coming from the other vantage point was the woman, also young at 70, who said, 'I've heard that veganism makes you so sensitive you can't live, but I don't agree with that. People become vegan because they *are* more sensitive.'

Once the step has been taken, what makes an 'ideal vegan?' I put that question to Chris and Gill Langley, a young couple for whom I feel a particular affinity. They both hold Ph.D. degrees in physiology from Cambridge, yet gave up their professions in biological research when they seriously considered the animal suffering involved. To Chris Langley, archetypal vegans are those 'who see that their way of living works and don't have to prove it to other people. The proof comes from their inner glow, from knowing that they can live and do everything they want without exploiting.' The ideal vegan in his wife's eyes is

. . . someone who not only talks compassionately but lives compassionately. It's someone who wouldn't push getting on the underground train, who's concerned about people *and* animals. That person would be well-informed, wouldn't present a 'cranky' image that would turn somebody else off, and would set a good example of veganism by the way they live.

There is no 'absolute' vegan: vinyl shoes may be cut by a machine that has a leather belt on it; there is a minute amount of animal gelatin in photographic film. Anyone with feet has inadvertently stepped on insects, and in gardening even some vegans have on occasion – when companion planting, mulching and mental telepathy[23] have not kept their crops from being ravaged – regretfully resorted to non-toxic (to anyone but bugs) insecticides. Still, if the Langleys' verbal portraits do depict ideal vegans, there must be thousands.[24] Many who come very close I feel truly blessed to know.

11.

The Glorious Possibility

This compassion in action may be the glorious possibility that could protect our crowded, polluted planet from its most intelligent and dangerous inhabitants, man. We have knowledge rarely tempered with wisdom, and technological accomplishments often surpassing our sense of responsibility regarding them. Peace Pilgrim, a vegan 'itinerant mystic', walked through America with the message that world peace will only result from one peaceful person's 'infecting' another in a vast epidemic of spiritual wellness. She emphasized the need to be an integrated adult: physical growing up proceeds more or less on its own, but emotional growth takes some effort, and reaching spiritual maturity, humanhood in full flower, could just be the purpose of living at all; it is at least in the running as an answer for the Big Question of why we're here. Still, most of us never set this as even an elusive goal, or if we consider it at all, it winds up filed away under 'Later' along with buying life insurance and making a will. Many modern-day prophets, the ecologists and futurists, say that 'later' is already here, that our address is 'Powder Keg, Earth', ready to ignite in massive famine, nuclear war, and science fiction-style backlashes from Mother Nature, the likes of which even a Wells or a Huxley could not have imagined. There seem to be two basic responses to that sort of information: either 'Things are so bad it's no use; I don't intend to change,' or 'Things can't be that bad; I don't intend to change.'

Vegans seem rather to have said, 'Things are what they are; they will only get better if I change.' Instead of being discouraged by the enormity of ills besetting the world, they start by lessening animal suffering, and healing seems to spread in a rippling effect. Vegans are living what Dr Michael

Fox calls 'a Biospiritual Ethic'. He speaks of

... a vital human imperative to evolve beyond the limited ego-states of individual, corporation, nation and the like to a true sense of global community, an ecological awareness in which all men are of one earth and one mind, united in terms of the highest ethical values and rational conduct, as well as empathic compassion and reverence for all life.[1]

In my concentrated contact with vegans, this 'imperative evolution' was unmistakenly apparent. For an individual vegan, it's just life. Most do not appear to consider themselves part of 'a movement', although nearly all the ones I met do belong to the British or American Vegan Society. They are simply living in tune – with logic as they see it, morality as they perceive it and, some would add, the infinite; capitalize that if you like.

That this project has changed me personally is a fact. It is most apparent in my own gradual conversion to veganism in practice; but I also feel – if at times only slightly – a degree of calm not with me before. I think of it as the 'serenity of surrender': it is very relaxing to have called a truce with my conscience. A gem from Peace Pilgrim is, 'When you live up to the highest light you have, more light will be given to you.'[2] At this point, I am not sure whether to take that as a promise or a threat! I personally believe that veganism is part of an all-encompassing spiritual quest. Neither graduation nor laurel-resting is in sight: as long, for example, as migrant farm workers in my own dear country are subject to conditions which should long since have been relegated to history, my vegetable soup and fruit salad are not as 'vegan' as they might be. Therefore, along with an intensified inner peace, I feel a psychic energy impelling me to work for change in an outer way.

Veganism on the diet and products level, is challenging, even fun. The ultimate ethic of compassion as a lifestyle, however, means putting the Golden Rule to use when that comes naturally and when it doesn't. It goes without saying that I will not reach that end even half the time. That means making amends and starting again – hopefully with 'more light having been given me' in the meantime.

Notes

Chapter 1: The Ultimate Ethic

1. Peter Singer, *Animal Liberation: Towards an End to Man's Inhumanity to Animals* (Thorsons, 1983), p.96.

2. Stephen R. L. Clark, *The Moral Status of Animals* (Oxford: Oxford University Press, 1977), p.3.

3. Albert Schweitzer, 'The Ethic of Reverence for Life', trans. John Naish, quoted in Tom Regan and Peter Singer, eds., *Animal Rights and Human Obligations* (Englewood Cliffs, NJ: Prentice-Hall, 1976), p.136.

Chapter 2: Towards A Definition

1. *Dorland's Medical Dictionary*, 24th ed (1974), s.v. 'vegan'.

2. [Alex Hershaft], *Vegetarianism Like it Is* (Washington, DC: Vegetarian Information Service, n.d.), p.1.

3. There is now another category of ethical vegetarian as well, the person who eliminates meat and possibly other animal foods from his diet out of concern for malnourished and starving humans, recognizing the impracticality of an animal-oriented agriculture in a hungry world. (See Chapter 7, 'Hunger, Ecology, Peace'.)

4. G. Allan Henderson, 'The Four Pillars of Health', *The Vegan* III (Spring 1947): 1.

5. In the Draize eye test, 'A group of rabbits are restrained by stocks to prevent movement and a drop of the test substance is applied to one eye . . . the other being left untreated as a comparison. The extent of the injury caused to the treated eye is monitored over the next seven days and each test is 'scored' according to the severity of the eye damage caused. This may vary from mild irritation to redness, clouding of the cornea, discharge, ulceration

and blindness.' (Gill Langley, Ph.D., *Animals and Cosmetics – What Is the Connection?* London: British Union for the Abolition of Vivisection, 1980, p.1.) Humane and potentially more accurate *in vitro* (test tube) testing is gradually being introduced to replace that using animals. Much of this exploration of alternative methods has come in response to animal activists' outrage at the earlier procedures.

6. *The Vegan* II (Summer 1946): frontispiece.

7. *The Vegan* III (Spring 1947): frontispiece.

8. When 'The Vegan Society' is used henceforth, it will refer to the British organization as distinct from the American Vegan Society which will be so designated.

9. *The Vegan* XX (Spring 1964): frontispiece.

10. The honey issue remains controversial. Some vegans maintain that when honey is taken by a careful beekeeper who removes only the excess, a symbiotic relationship exists between man and bee, and no exploitation of the lower life form is taking place. Because commercial beekeeping involves removal of most of the honey and its replacement with an inferior corn syrup substitute, and because the bees are often killed by rough handling, most vegans choose to do without the sweetener. I surveyed forty vegans on this; only nine use honey and these are careful to 'know the source' of the product.

11. *The Vegan* XXVII (Spring 1980): frontispiece.

12. Eva Batt, *Why Veganism?* (Malaga, NJ: American Vegan Society, n.d.), p.2.

Chapter 3: Reverence for Life: Schweitzer and Christianity

1. Albert Schweitzer, quoted in H. Jay Dinshah, ed., *Here's Harmlessness* (Malaga, NJ: American Vegan Society, 1973), p.5.

2. Ibid.

3. Schweitzer, 'The Ethic of Reference for Life', trans. John Naish, quoted in Tom Regan and Peter Singer, eds., *Animal Rights and Human Obligations* (Englewood Cliffs, NJ: Prentice-Hall, 1976), p.136.

4. Charles R. Joy, trans. and ed., *The Animal World of Albert Schweitzer: Jungle Insights into Reverence for Life* (Boston: Beacon Press, 1950), pp.19-20.

5. Schweitzer, 'The Ethic of Reverence for Life', quoted in Regan and Singer (see note 3), pp.133-4.

6. Ibid.

7. Quotations from persons interviewed personally by myself and information from those who completed my questionnaires during my research period will henceforth not be footnoted.

8. Revd V. A. Holmes-Gore, *These We Have Not Loved, A Treatise on the Christian Attitude to the Creatures* (London: C. D. Daniel, 1941), p.27.

9. Andrew Linzey, 'Animals and Moral Theology (1)', quoted in David Paterson and Richard D. Ryder, eds., *Animal Rights – A Symposium* (Fontwell, Sussex: Centaur Press, 1979), pp.34-6.

10. Dudley Giehl, *Vegetarianism, A Way of Life*, with a foreword by Isaac Bashevis Singer (New York: Harper & Row, 1979), p.200.

11. Eric Turnbill, 'Animals and Moral Theology (2)', quoted in Paterson and Ryder (see note 9), pp.45-46.

12. Irish Catholic Study Circle for Animal Welfare, '1979 Annual Report', p.1. (Mimeographed.)

13. Stephen Gaskin, quoted by Kathleen Jannaway in my 13 June 1980 interview with her in Leatherhead, Surrey.

14. Anna Kingsford, quoted in John Vyvyan, *In Pity and In Anger, A Study of the Use of Animals in Science* (London: Michael Joseph, 1969), p.151.

Chapter 4: Gandhi, Eastern Thought and Ahimsa

1. H. Jay Dinshah, *Out of the Jungle*, 4th edn (Malaga, NJ: American Vegan Society, 1975), p.19.

2. Mahatma Gandhi, quoted in 'You Are What You Eat', *East-West Journal*, June 1980, p.37.

3. Gandhi, quoted in Dinshah, *Here's Harmlessness* (Malaga, NJ: American Vegan Society, 1973), p.13.

4. Paramahansa Yogananda, *Autobiography of a Yogi*, 14th edn (Los Angeles: Self-Realization Fellowship, 1971), pp.443-4.

5. *How to Know God, the Yoga Aphorisms of Patanjali*, trans. and with commentary by Swami Prabhavananda and Christopher Isherwood (Hollywood: Vedanta Press, 1953), p.147.

6. *The Song of God, Bhagavad-Gita*, trans. by Prabhavananda and Isherwood (New York: New American Library, 1972), p.61.

7. Ibid., p.67.

8. Ibid., p.99.

9. Yogananda, pp.50-1.

10. John B. Noss, *Man's Religions*, 5th edn (New York: Macmillan, 1974), p.112.

11. Mahavira, quoted in Dinshah, *Here's Harmlessness*, p.15.

12. Results of thirty-five vegans' being asked, 'What religion do you feel comes closest to vegan principles?' were: Don't know, 11; Buddhism, 9; No religion comes close, 5; Hinduism, 4; Miscellaneous (the Atlanteans, the Order of the Cross, and 'the non-institutional religion of "brotherhood and sisterhood"'), 3; Society of Friends, 2; Seventh-Day Adventists, 1.

13. Clarence H. Hamilton, ed., *Buddhism, A Religion of Infinite Compassion, Selections from Buddhist Literature* (Indianapolis: Bobbs-Merrill, 1952), p.112.

14. The Buddha, quoted in Dinshah, *Here's Harmlessness*, p.9.

15. Ibid.

16. Bhagwan Shree Rajnessh, 'The Spiritual Side of Vegetarianism', *Vegetarian Times*, March 1980, p.64.

17. 'The Pillars of Ahimsa' are descriptions of the concept using each letter of the Sanskrit term to define a facet of it. Elaboration on these comprise a section of H. Jay Dinshah's *Out of the Jungle* (see note 1), pp.18-26; that section was also published separately as a booklet, *The Pillars of Ahimsa* (Malaga, NJ: American Vegan Society, 1975).

18. John A. Hardon, S. J., *Religions of the Orient, A Christian View* (Chicago: Loyola University Press, 1970), p.175.

19. Mark Bowden, 'The Modern Test-Tube Cow', *East-West Journal*, June 1980, p.32.

20. Ibid., p.33.

21. Dinshah, *Out of the Jungle*, p.21.

22. Ibid., p.27.

23. Noss (see note 10), p.224.

Chapter 5: Humans and Other Animals

1. Martin Luther King, Jr., quoted in H. Jay Dinshah, *Here's Harmlessness* (Malaga, NJ: American Vegan Society, 1973), p.26.

2. Richard Claxton Gregory, *Dick Gregory's Natural Diet for Folks Who Eat: Cookin' With Mother Nature* (New York: Perennial Library, 1974), pp.15-16.

3. Nathaniel Altman, *Eating for Life*, rev. edn, with a preface by

Geoffrey Hodson (Wheaton, Ill.: Quest Books, 1977), p.6.

4. Ibid.

5. Ella Wheeler Wilcox, quoted in ibid., p.143.

6. Victor Hugo, quoted in John Vyvyan, *The Dark Face of Science* (London: Michael Joseph, 1971), pp.105-6.

7. Leonardo da Vinci, quoted in Dinshah (see note 1), p.47.

8. Henry David Thoreau, quoted in ibid., p.41.

9. Count Leo Tolstoy, quoted in ibid., p.17.

10. Altman (see note 3), p.141.

11. Percy Bysshe Shelley, quoted in ibid., pp.141-2.

12. Books by Jon Wynne-Tyson which deal with the ideals behind compassionate living and veganism include *The Civilized Alternative, A Pattern for Protest* (Fontwell, Sussex: Centaur Press, 1972), and *Food for a Future, the Complete Case for Vegetarianism*, London: Centaur Press, 1979). See 'Additional Recommended Reading'.

13. Stephen Kellert, 'Attitudes Toward Animals', *Vegetarian Times*, Sept.-Oct. 1978, p.15.

14. Ibid., pp.16-19.

15. Ibid., p.23.

16. A useful resource on feeding dogs and cats is *Bone Appétit! Natural Foods for Pets*, by Frances Sheridan Goulart (Seattle WA: Pacific Search Books, 1976), although it is not completely vegetarian. Additional information on vegetarian feeding of pets may be obtained from World of God, Inc., Box 1418, Umatilla, Fla. 32784, USA; this small religious group is vegan and their *Cookbook for People Who Love Animals* contains a chapter of vegan recipes for pets. This author knows personally of some dogs who are thriving on vegetarian diets, but cats so nourished are more difficult to find. Some reports state that severe health problems, notably blindness, can result when cats are given no flesh foods. Others assert that vegetarian cats are catching a mouse on the sly now and again and therefore cannot be seen as really vegetarian. Still, there have been healthy vegetarian cats: theosophical writer Norman Pearson had such a pet for many years and included a photograph of her in his book, *Space, Time, and Self*. The Vegetarian Society of the UK has a valuable leaflet on this subject as well. There is also an account of a voluntarily vegetarian lioness in the book, *Little Tyke* by Georges Westbeau (Mountain View, CA: Pacific Press Publ. Assn.).

17. A non-vegetarian book dealing with the welfare of non-

agricultural animals is *Man Kind?* by Cleveland Amory (New York: Harper & Row, 1974).

Chapter 6: The Vegan Stand

1. Tom Regan, quoted in Tom Regan and Peter Singer, eds., *Animal Rights and Human Obligations* (Englewood Cliffs, NJ: Prentice-Hall, 1976), p.4.

2. John Harris, *Vegetarianism: The Ethics* (Altrincham, Cheshire: the Vegetarian Society (UK), 1978), p.3.

3. Dan Freeman, *The Great Apes* (New York: G. P. Putnam's Sons, 1979), p.126.

4. Ibid., p.73.

5. Ibid., p.92.

6. Nathaniel Altman, *Eating for Life*, rev. edn, with a preface by Geoffrey Hodson (Wheaton, Ill.: Quest Books, 1977), pp.77-9.

7. Ibid., pp.76-7.

8. Ibid., p.75. (Sources: US per capita meat consumption statistics for 1976, and average dressed weights of slaughtered animals from *Livestock and Meat Statistics*, US Dept. of Agriculture.)

9. Peter Singer, *Animal Liberation: Towards an End to Man's Inhumanity to Animals* (Thorsons, 1983), p.96.

10. Dr T. R. Preston, quoted in Ruth Harrison, *Animal Machines* (London: Vincent Stuart, 1964), p.1.

11. James B. Mason, 'Industrial Pigs, Mechanical Chickens: How Corporate Animal Factories Breed Poisoned Meat and New Pollution', *Vegetarian Times*, March 1980, p.52.

12. Brigid Brophy, quoted in Dudley Giehl, *Vegetarianism, A Way of Life*, with a foreword by Isaac Bashevis Singer (New York: Harper & Row, 1979), p.61.

13. James Kovik and Mary Jo Kovik, *The True Facts on Slaughter for Sport* (Baltimore: Defenders of Animal Rights, 1977), pp.1-2, 6. At the Hanford Reservation in the northwestern USA, hunting was banned in 1943 without harm to native deer or their predators. At the Great Swamp Wildlife Refuge in New Jersey where there are no natural predators, rifle groups lobbied for an end to a four-year moratorium on hunting that they might reduce a supposed overpopulation of starving deer. After the killing, not one deer was found in a condition of starvation and 90 per cent had moderate to excellent quantities of fat.

14. Mark Braunstein, 'On Being Radically Vegetarian', *Vegetarian Times*, March 1980, p.72.

15. Eva Batt, *Why Veganism?* (Malaga, NJ: American Vegan Society, n.d.), pp.3-4.

16. 'Report of the Brambell Committee', H. M. Stationery Office, 1965, quoted in [Kathleen Jannaway], *What Happens to the Calf?* (Leatherhead, Surrey: the Vegan Society, 1975), p.1.

17. Singer, *Animal Liberation* (see note 9), p.129.

18. [Jannaway], pp.1-3.

19. Jon A. Jackson, 'The Life and Death of an American Chicken', *Saturday Review*, 2 Sept. 1972, p.12.

20. Singer, *Animal Liberation* (see note 9), p.114.

21. *Poultry Tribune*, Feb. 1974, quoted in ibid., p.111.

22. Harrison, *Animal Machines* (see note 10), p.48.

23. 'Report of the Brambell Committee', quoted in Singer, *Animal Liberation*, p.104.

24. Singer, *Animal Liberation* (see note 9), pp.111-12.

Chapter 7: Hunger, Ecology, Peace

1. Vic Sussman, *The Vegetarian Alternative, A Guide to a Healthful and Humane Diet* (Emmaus, Pa.: Rodale Press, 1978), p.239.

2. Addeke H. Boerma, quoted in Nathaniel Altman, *Eating for Life*, rev. edn, with a preface by Geoffrey Hodson (Wheaton, Ill.: Quest Books, 1975), p.40.

3. Frances Moore Lappé, *Diet for a Small Planet*, rev. edn (New York: Ballantine Books, 1975), p.40.

4. Ibid., p.11. (Source: USDA Economic Resources Services, Beltsville, Md.)

5. Jack Lucas, *Vegetarianism: The World Food Problem* (Altrincham, Cheshire: the Vegetarian Society (UK) 1978), p.6.

6. Lappé (see note 3), p.10.

7. K. E. Hunt, Director, Institute of Agrarian Affairs, Oxford, quoted in Altman, *Eating for Life*, p.53.

8. Altman (see note 2), p.53.

9. Jon Wynne-Tyson, *Food for a Future, the Complete Case for Vegetarianism* (New York: Universe Books, 1979), p.16.

10. Aaron M. Altschul, quoted in Altman, p.60.

11. Altman (see note 2), p.58.

12. Ibid., p.57.

13. Serena Coles, 'Blueprint for a Humane World', paper presented at the 23rd World Vegetarian Congress (International Vegetarian Union), University of Maine at Orono, 23 August 1975.

14. Lester Brown, quoted in Sussman (see note 1), p.238.

15. Lappé (see note 3), pp.5-6.

16. Sussman (see note 1), p.234.

17. The Vegan Society, 'Food for a Future' (leaflet) (Leatherhead, Surrey: the Vegan Society, n.d.).

18. Louis H. Bean, quoted by Altman (see note 2), p.54.

19. Altman (see note 2), p.54.

20. For detailed information on veganic gardening, see 'The Garden of Ahimsa', in H. Jay Dinshah, ed., *Here's Harmlessness* (Malaga, NJ: American Vegan Society, 1973).

21. Henry Bailey Stevens, quoted in Dinshah (see note 20), p.9.

22. Ibid.

23. George Bernard Shaw, quoted in Coles, *Blueprint for a Humane World*.

24. Stephen R. L. Clark, *The Moral Status of Animals* (Oxford: Oxford University Press, 1977), p.17.

Chapter 8: Making the Break

1. Peter Singer, *Animal Liberation: Towards an End to Man's Inhumanity to Animals* (Thorsons, 1983), p.96, pp.191-2.

2. Frances Moore Lappé, *Diet for a Small Planet*, rev. edn (New York: Ballantine Books, 1975), p.143.

3. H. Jay Dinshah, *How to be a Total-Vegetarian* (Malaga, NJ: American Vegan Society, 1975), p.5.

4. Jo Hicks and John Hicks, 'Why *We're* Vegan', *The Vegan* XXVI (Summer 1979): 30.

5. Miso is a matured bean and grain paste indigenous to Japan. It is salty and thus makes a savoury base for soups, generally with the addition of onion, carrot and other vegetables; it is also used in dips, spreads, etc.

6. Tofu is soya bean cake or soya bean curd. It can be made at home

from the beans or from soya flour in rather the way one would make cottage cheese from milk, but it is now widely available at supermarkets and natural food shops, usually cut into cubes. By itself, tofu is a bland white substance of thick gelatin consistency, but it may be seasoned for a variety of dishes. With the addition of soya sauce, garlic, or herbs, it can be turned into 'steaks' or 'burgers', scrambled like eggs, blended as a creamy salad dressing or mashed as a dip, but with the addition of sweetener (dates, maple syrup, etc.), it becomes the base for desserts such as puddings and cheesecake. Replaces cheese in many recipes.

7. Carob powder is the starchy, chocolate-flavoured ground pod of the locust bean. It is also called 'St John's bread' because the 'locusts' John the Baptist supposedly ate in the desert ('. . . he did eat locusts and wild honey', Mark 1:6; '. . . and his meat was locusts and wild honey', Matthew 3:4) were not insects but the locust beans. The powder, available at health food shops, can be substituted for cocoa or chocolate; carob bars and other prepared sweets made from carob are also on the market.

8. Muesli is a near-classic food reform cereal which supposedly originated at the Bircher-Benner Sanitarium in Switzerland. Its base is uncooked oats soaked overnight; in the morning, grated raw apple and chopped or ground hazelnuts are added, and a milk or juice topping. Other fruits or nuts may be used, and wheatgerm is sometimes sprinkled on as well.

9. 'Barmene', 'Natex' and 'Tastex' are B_{12}-fortified; 'Marmite' is an unfortified but readily available brand popular throughout England. In the USA powdered nutritional yeast, many varieties of which are B_{12}-fortified, is more widely used than yeast extract, although extract is sold under the brand names 'Sovex' and 'Vegex'.

10. When a vegan has cereal, it is be topped with commercial plant milk (England's 'Plamil', 'Granogen' or Golden Archer 'Beanmilk'; or 'Soyamel', 'Soyagen' or 'Soymoo' in the USA), a homemade soya or nutmilk (see Recipes), fruit juice or blended banana.

11. The vegan stance on health, healing and health practitioners and preparations is covered in Chapter 10, 'A Holistic Look at Health and Vegans'.

12. Dinshah (see note 3), p.9.

13. Ibid.

14. Eva Batt, *Wool Factories* (Leatherhead, Surrey: The Vegan Society, n.d.), pp.2-4.

15. Marjorie Osborn, comp. and ed., *More Than Skin Deep* (Tunbridge Wells, Kent: Beauty Without Cruelty, 1975), p.6.

16. Gill Langley, Ph.D., *Animals and Cosmetics – What Is The Connection?* (London: British Union for the Abolition of Vivisection, 1980, p.1.

17. Osborn (see note 15), p.24.

18. Vegan food is very inexpensive; only nuts are costly and they are concentrated foods eaten in small amounts. Some of the money saved on grocery bills does have to go for vegan commodities that are sometimes more expensive because there is not a large demand for them (health food soaps and toothpaste, for example), but in total, veganism is an extremely economical manner of living.

Chapter 9: Nutritional Considerations

1. Frances Moore Lappé, *Diet for a Small Planet*, rev. edn (New York, Ballantine Books, 1975), p.81.

2. Ralph Cinqué, D.C., quoted in Victoria Moran, 'The Self-Healing Body: A Look at the Theory of Natural Hygiene', *Vegetarian Times*, July 1980, p.52.

3. Julian Whitaker, M.D., 'Vegan Diet in Cardio-Vascular Disease Therapy', address presented at the North American Vegetarian Society Annual Conference, Earlham College, Richmond, Ind., 12 July 1980.

4. Nathaniel Altman, *Eating for Life*, rev. edn., with a preface by Geoffrey Hodson (Wheaton, Ill.: Quest Books, 1977), p.105. Source: B. K. Watt and A. L. Merrill, *Composition of Foods* (Washington: USDA, 1963), the source for nutritional content of foods given in this chapter unless otherwise noted.

5. T. A. B. Sanders, Ph.D., and Frey R. Ellis, M.D., *Vegan Nutrition* (Leatherhead, Surrey: The Vegan Society, 1979), p.18.

6. A. D. M. Smith, quoted in Richard Bargen, M.D., *The Vegetarian's Self-Defense Manual* (Wheaton, Ill.: Quest Books, 1979), p.86.

Chapter 10: A Holistic Look at Health and Vegans

1. [Alex Hershaft], *Vegetarianism Like it Is* (Washington, DC: Vegetarian Information Service, n.d.), p.1.

2. Julian Whitaker, M.D., "Vegan Diet in Cardio-Vascular Disease Therapy', address presented at the North American Vegetarian Society Annual Conference, Earlham College, Richmond, Ind., 12 July 1980.

3. Editorial: 'Diet and Stress in Vascular Disease', *Journal of the American Medical Association* 176(9) (1961): 806-7.

4. Dr Raymond J. Shamberger, quoted by Nathaniel Altman, *Eating for Life*, rev. edn., with a preface by Geoffrey Hodson (Wheaton, Ill.: Quest Books, 1977), p.47.

5. Vic Sussman, *The Vegetarian Alternative, A Guide to a Healthful and Humane Diet* (Emmaus, Pa.: Rodale Press, 1978), p.156.

6. Ibid., pp.155-6.

7. D. D. MacKinsey, quoted in Altman, *Eating for Life* (see note 4), p.42.

8. Altman, *Eating for Life* (see note 4), p.50.

9. See Frances Moore Lappé, *Diet for a Small Planet*, rev. edn, (New York: Ballantine Books, 1975), pp.31-40; also, Altman (see note 4), pp.42-3; and Sussman (see note 5), pp.154-75.

10. Eva Batt, *Why Veganism?* (Malaga, NJ: American Vegan Society, n.d.), p.9.

11. Frey R. Ellis, M.D., quoted in *A Better Future for All Life* (London: British Broadcasting Corpn, film series: 'The Open Door', n.d.).

12. Patrick K. Moran, 'Vegetarianism and the Cardio-Vascular System' (Master's thesis, University of Missouri at Kansas City, 1975), pp.35-7.

13. Altman (see note 4), p.150.

14. Rob Allanson, 'Cutting Through the Cream Cheese', *East-West Journal*, June 1980, pp.52-3.

15. See Chapter 11, 'Rearing Vegan Children'.

16. Altman (see note 4), p.150.

17. Carl G. Jung, quoted in John Vyvyan, *The Dark Face of Science* (London: Michael Joseph, 1971), p.46.

18. Harry Bonnie, letter to the editor, *The Vegan* XVI (Summer 1969): 26.

19. Serena Coles, letter to the editor, *The Vegan* XVI (Summer 1969): 26.

20. Thomas A. Edison, quoted in *Nutritional Perspectives* III (April 1980): back cover.

21. Stephen R. L. Clark, *The Moral Status of Animals* (Oxford: Oxford University Press, 1977), p.19.

22. Leo Tolstoy, quoted in H. Jay Dinshah, ed., *Here's Harmlessness* (Malaga, NJ: American Vegan Society, 1973), p.17.

23. Telepathic communication with non-humans is dealt with in J. Allen Boone, *The Language of Silence* (New York: Harper & Row, 1970); and also in Muriel, the Lady Dowding, 'Co-operation', quoted in Dinshah (see note 22), p.18: 'My husband, Lord Dowding, once spoke in the House of Lords about the Cruel Poisons Bill and mentioned this method of controlling animals. It was received in shocked silence by their Lordships. But the press swooped down on us with joy . . . The outcome of this was that many people who did not like putting mouse-traps or poisons down, tried this method in desperation, not really believing it could possibly work, and then wrote to tell us that they had found to their amazement that it did!'

24. The actual number of intentional vegans (that is, those who choose to be vegan, not the millions who use no animal products because poverty has taken the choice away) is difficult to estimate. *The Vegan* has over 7,000 subscribers in twenty-six countries; some of these are associate members (not fully practising vegans), but The Vegan Society estimates that in England alone there is at least one vegan who does not belong to the Society for every one that does, and many more are 'near vegans'. A 1978 Roper Poll in the USA estimated that 9-10 million Americans consider themselves vegetarian; the number of vegans among them is unknown.

Chapter 11: The Glorious Possibility

1. Michael W. Fox, M.D., Ph.D., D.V.M., 'What Future for Man and Earth? Towards a Biospiritual Ethic', quoted in Richard Knowles Morris and Michael W. Fox, eds., *On the Fifth Day: Animal Rights and Human Ethics* (Washington, D.C.: Acropolis Books, 1978), p.220.

2. Wisdom of Peace Pilgrim has been collected in *Peace Pilgrim; Her Life and Work in Her Own Words*. (Santa Fe, NM: Ocean Tree Books, 1983). Available for only a postage donation is the booklet *Steps Toward Inner Peace* from Friends of Peace Pilgrim, 43480 Cedar Ave., Hemet, CA 92343. Cassette tapes are also offered for sale.

Part 2

12.
Rearing Vegan Children

More and more orthodox nutritionists are coming to sanction dietary veganism for adults, but many still warn against it for growing children. They are evidently not aware of the three-generation evidence of healthy vegan families in Britain and elsewhere. They do, however, know of studies which have reported protein malnutrition and other dire effects to children on what were called vegan diets. The regimens on which these children were existing, though, bear virtually no resemblance to the balanced, varied food plan recommended by The Vegan Society. They were instead bizarre cult diets consisting of such restricted fare as all brown rice or all tree fruit. It is indeed unfortunate that sensible veganism is confused with such extremism, especially since quality vegan diets mean fewer allergies, less obesity, and other health benefits for children.

In any case, the nutrients which some dieticians fear that vegan children will lack are those which conventional eaters largely obtain from animal products: protein, iron, calcium, riboflavin, vitamin D and vitamin B_{12}. Conscientious vegan parents realize that some planning is needed to ensure that these and other factors are present in the family diet, but surely omnivorous and lacto-ovo-vegetarian parents must plan nutritious meals, too. Protein-rich snacks – nuts, seeds, tofu dip for crisps, homemade soya milk or commercial plant milk (Plamil, Granogen, Golden Archer Beanmilk, Provamel, etc.) – are usually available for vegan youngsters. Many homemakers also practise protein complementation. This combining of nuts or seeds with legumes or leafy vegetables, or of legumes with grains, is said to enhance the usability by the body of available amino acids, the building blocks of protein. (This is treated fully in Lappé's *Diet for a Small Planet* listed in the Bibliography. Some feel that the theory is groundless and supports the misguided notion that plant protein must mimic that of animal origin; this is detailed in *A Vegetarian Sourcebook* on the list of 'Additional Recommended Reading'.)

Foods that vegans eat routinely are often absent from other households. There can be little worry of insufficient iron intake when a child (or adult) is eating pulses, dates and dried apricots, blackstrap molasses, soya products and wheatgerm. The calcium milk-drinkers get in dairy goods is available in dark leafy greens, almonds, carob, pulses, corn tortillas, sesame, tofu and fortified plant milks; riboflavin is found in leafy greens, legumes and whole grains. Additional calcium is sometimes given to children in supplement form, as is vitamin D when abundant year-round sunshine is not available. B_{12} is also supplemented or provided through consistent use of fortified yeast extracts and commercial plantmilks. A regular multivitamin/mineral provides a bit of 'nutrition insurance' for any child, particularly those with small appetites.

Even before taking his place at the family table, the vegan baby can get a very good start in life. His mother is apt to avoid harmful substances like drugs and chemicals as a matter of course, making his antenatal environment a safer one. Her diet is rich in vital folic acid, and she is likely to be especially careful to get the additional calories, protein, iron and calcium needed during pregnancy. When she is breast-feeding, she puts her child at a distinct advantage since her milk is far lower in pesticide residues than that of other mothers. If she continues with her antenatal vitamin/mineral supplement, takes in sufficient calories and plenty of fluids, she should have no trouble nursing for a year or longer. During that time, her baby is automatically protected from the allergy common in infants to dairy products consumed by their mothers. If breast-feeding must end early or is for some reason not undertaken, soya-based infant formulas can be substituted. These are *not* the same as commercial plant milks meant for adults and older children but are rather designed to simulate mother's milk as closely as possible to provide total nutrition for an infant.

Children past babyhood will need an abundance of quality protein to satisfy their growth needs, as well as plenty of caloric energy, all the vitamins, calcium for bone development, and other minerals. Parents can meet these requirements by providing fresh, natural foods in quantity, particularly leafy greens (in salads, juices, or lightly cooked). Variety in the concentrated foodstuffs (grains, beans, dried fruits) is also important, and B_{12} in some form is mandatory. With these guidelines, only the allergic child or the very finicky eater would give parents cause for real concern. A vegan child allergic to soya or wheat would have a limited diet unless his or her caretakers put forth the effort to provide ample replacements of other legumes and grains. Fortunately, allergies do not appear with great frequency in vegan children, due in part at least to breast-feeding and avoidance of the premature introduction of solid foods to infants.

As for the child who is extremely fussy about his food, attractive dishes and an unruffled parental posture go far towards making meals more appealing. This problem seems to occur less frequently in vegan households than in others, perhaps because wholesome fare has made up the menu from toddlerhood, because fresh air and exercise have produced keen appetites, or that the children's tastes have not been perverted by vast amounts of sweets. (So many commercial sweets and pastries include dairy products, eggs, and/or animal fat that vegans generally make their own desserts and snacks, often using sugar minimally or substituting dates, maple syrup or other natural sweeteners.)

As the child grows, social considerations become almost as crucial as the nutritional ones. Here parents vary widely in their approach. Many allow their children the freedom to eat whatever is offered when they are with friends. Given this opportunity to choose, the children either refuse non-vegan items because they themselves believe in veganism, or they are comfortable with a compromise to vegetarian foods. Parents are challenged to make vegan meals and treats tempting and tasty enough to keep such compromises to a minimum. They realize, however, the tremendous pressure on children to be like their peers, and they never treat veganism as a deprivation. It is seen instead as an active way to participate in kindness to animals, part of a total lifestyle emphasizing gentleness and caring.

The most reassuring thing a vegan parent can remember is that this has been done before, and done most successfully. The children and grandchildren of the Vegan Society's pioneers are, both physically and emotionally, the finest examples of the lifestyle's efficacy. The stories of some of these are told in the two booklets entitled *Vegan Mothers and Children* put out by The Vegan Society. The following are also helpful resources:

Dinshah, Freya, 'Feeding Vegan Babies', *Ahimsa*, January/March 1982. Malaga, New Jersey: the American Vegan Society.

Howard, Frances, and Friedenstern Howard. *Parents' Handbook of Breastfeeding and Plant Foods*. 38 Hampden Road, Hitchin, Herts.: Mr and Mrs F. Howard, 1975.

Shandler, Mike, and Nina Shandler. *The Complete Guide and Cookbook to Raising Your Child as a Vegetarian*. New York: Ballantine Books, 1982.

Yntema, Sharon. *Vegetarian Baby*. Ithaca, New York: McBooks Press, 1980.

The most crucial point to keep in mind is that veganism is much more than a diet. When children are brought up in an atmosphere in which reverence for all life is both taught and practised, they often become its staunchest advocates. A love for animals comes naturally to most little ones. In a vegan home, this love is respected, nurtured, and allowed to grow to the fullest.

13.

Slimming on a Vegan Diet

Oftentimes new vegans find a welcome loss of unwanted weight after they've been off all animal products for a few weeks or months. The serendipitous dimension of this is that it's happened without effort and certainly without hunger. When the high-fat foods like pork, beef, whole milk and hard cheese are replaced by vegetables and grains with their bulk and non-caloric fibre, one's daily calorie intake is lowered dramatically without a loss of satiety.

For the 'professional slimmer', however, things aren't always so simple. She – and it is usually a woman – has already exchanged fatty meats for lean ones, switched to skimmed milk, and eaten her eggs poached or hard-boiled. She has read so much about high protein weight loss diets that the very thought of going without broiled fish and cottage cheese is close to terrifying. The very word 'carbohydrate' strikes terror in her soul, and the vegan diet is rich in natural carbohydrates. A bit of re-education will be necessary for this person to undertake the change to veganism without a nagging fear for her figure.

That re-education can begin with a renewed look at the protein question. The animal foods high in protein have been touted by advertisers as a boon for slimmers, but the truth is that any calories ingested over the amount burned for energy and for carrying on life processes will be stored as fat. This is the case for the calories in protein as well as those in carbohydrates (starches and sugars) and those in fats. The calorific cost of a gram of protein is virtually identical to that of a gram of carbohydrate – about four – while the calories in fat are more than double that at nine per gram. Almost any vegan diet is low in fat, so the weight-watcher enters veganism with that bonus awaiting her.

The complex carbohydrate found in whole grains, pulses, vegetables and fresh fruit is a friend to the dieter as well. Unlike simple sugars (white or brown sugar, honey, syrups) and refined starches (white flour, white rice, degerminated maize meal), these foods from Mother Nature digest slowly and keep the blood sugar level – one important appetite indicator – reasonably stable.

The dark leafy greens, lauded so often for their nutritional largesse, are also excellent for anyone keeping tabs on the waistline. Other vegetables, too, are notoriously calorie-shy. Tofu is a splendid vegan protein food low in both fat and calories, and textured vegetable proteins, such as the totally vegan variety by Lotus Foods, are also useful in creating satisfying entrées for the dieter. Fresh fruits make healthy and refreshing desserts. (The consistent vegan would likely eschew artificial sweeteners due to its history of laboratory tests using animals.)

For someone serious about losing weight, the concentrated vegan foods would need to be consumed only moderately. These include nuts (having on hand only nuts in their shells is a trick some slimmers use), dried fruits (very sweet and in no way necessary if fresh fruit is eaten), oils and margarine. Even so, one look at vegans themselves should be sufficient to convince any sceptic: it is close to impossible to find an obese vegan. I am inclined to think that this results both from their diet and from their attitude. They are simply too busy working for a better world to have time for destructive habits like overeating! There is also a keen appreciation for life, nature and vitality among them, so exercise and fresh air outings are a part of most vegans' routines.

Chronic addiction to excess food is a real and dangerous problem. 'I tried for years to be vegan', an attractive young woman told me, 'but I'd always break down with a candy bar and then eat everything in sight. Or I'd tell myself that since I wasn't eating so many other foods, I could stuff myself with all the nuts and dates and raisins I could hold. It was a nightmare. I had to come to grips with my overeating problem first, and realize that I couldn't 'control' food, vegan or not. It took a couple of years to get help with that before I could attempt veganism again. I did, and it's lasted. A lot of vegans think I was terribly selfish to use animal products after I had learned of the cruelties involved, but I had to get myself together before I could help anyone else, people or animals. For me, it had to be a slow process.'

Group support can be useful when the difficulty is severe. Overeaters Anonymous has helped some vegans who appreciate the fellowship because of its emphasis on the underlying emotional causes of one's abuse of food. It backs no specific diet, so vegans can feel comfortable and accepted within the group and meet no opposition to their chosen style of eating. (For the meeting location in your area, write to O.A. World Service, 2190 190th St, Torrance, California 90504, USA. There is no charge for membership.)

For those simply interested in a bit of girth control, these calorie-counted recipes can be a delicious introduction to slimming vegan style.

LOW CALORIE VEGAN RECIPES

Tofu Mayonnaise Dressing or Dip

6 oz (170g) tofu, drained
2 tablespoonsful lemon juice
2 tablespoonsful vegetable oil
½ teaspoonful salt
Dash ground black pepper
1 tablespoonful parsley, finely chopped

1. Purée all the ingredients in blender until smooth (about 30 seconds).

Note: May be varied with the addition of 2 oz diced onion, a garlic clove, or ¼ teaspoonful dillweed. Yields approximately 8 oz and provides 160 calories. (Ordinary mayonnaise has 1,580 calories per 8 oz.) Good vegetables for 'skinny dipping' include raw courgettes, cauliflower, broccoli, carrot sticks, celery, mushrooms, Jerusalem artichokes, asparagus tips and tender stalks, and strips of green and red pepper.

Waist-Watching Herb Dressing

4 tablespoonsful olive oil
4 tablespoonsful apple cider vinegar
1 tablespoonful prepared mustard
1 tablespoonful lemon juice
1 tablespoonful chopped parsley
1 tablespoonful chopped chives
½ teaspoonful basil
Pinch of cayenne pepper
1 clove garlic, pressed
6oz (170g) tomato juice

1. Combine all the ingredients and mix well.

Note: Makes ½ pint (285ml), with 33 calories per tablespoonful. Wonderful on greens – particularly good after standing in fridge a few hours to blend flavours.

Clever Quiche
Serves 4

For crust:
½lb (455g) uncooked short-grain brown rice
½ teaspoonful sea salt
¾ pint (425ml) water
1 teaspoonful vegetable oil

For filling:
1 medium onion, chopped
2oz (55g) mushrooms, sliced
2 cloves garlic, diced
4 tablespoonsful water
1lb (455g) tofu
2 tablespoonsful soya sauce (tamari)

1. Make the crust as follows. Put rice and salt in pan with water and bring to low boil. Cover and cook for 30 minutes, stirring occasionally. (The cooked rice should be sticky.)

2. While rice is cooking, simmer onion, mushrooms and garlic in water for 5 minutes or until water has evaporated.

3. Grate half the tofu and put the rest in blender with soya sauce.

4. Add vegetable mixture and grated tofu to blended mixture.

5. Oil a 9-inch pie tin and press the cooked rice firmly into it. Add filling and bake 20-30 minutes at 350°F/180°C (Gas Mark 4). Let stand 5 minutes before serving.

Note: Crust may be pre-cooked and refrigerated. Each serving of quiche is approximately 215 calories and has only 6.12g of fat.

Slim Vegetable Curry
Serves 4

½ teaspoonful curry powder
½ pint (285ml) tomato sauce
2 oz (55g) aubergine, cut in 1-inch cubes
1 lb (455g) courgettes, chopped
4 oz (115g) mushrooms, quartered
1½ oz (45g) tofu, cut in 1-inch cubes
1 oz (30g) chopped walnuts, almonds or cashews
2 tablespoonsful sunflower seeds
2 tablespoonsful chopped chives
2 tablespoonsful chopped parsley

1. In frying pan or large saucepan, blend curry powder into tomato sauce. Add aubergine and pepper. Cover and cook 5-8 minutes, stirring occasionally. (Add water if necessary to keep sauce moist and avoid sticking.)

2. Add courgettes; cover and cook 5 minutes.

3. Add other ingredients. Mix well. Cover and cook 2 minutes more until mushrooms are hot and done, yet crisp.

Note: 200 calories per serving.

Light Gazpacho (Chilled Mexican Soup)
Serves 2

1 medium tomato, peeled and diced
¼ large cucumber, peeled and chopped
¼ large green pepper, seeded
2 slices onion
2 sprigs parsley

1. Combine and liquify all ingredients in blender.
Note: ⅓ pint (200ml) and 50 calories per serving.

Slender Shake
Serves 1

12 blanched almonds
1 small ripe banana
⅓ pint (200ml) water
4 ice cubes
Dash vanilla
Dash nutmeg

1. Combine and liquify all ingredients in blender.

2. Serve over ice.

Note: Makes ¾ pint (425ml), 124 calories.

See general recipes in the next chapter for more ideas. You might also wish to read Leah Leneman's 1980 paperback *Slimming the Vegetarian Way*, published by Thorsons.

14.

Recipes

The real stars of a vegan table are simple, natural foods: vegetables, fruits, nuts and grains. These items are colourful and enticing in themselves and can be enjoyed with a minimum of preparation. The people who change over to veganism from conventional living or lacto-ovo-vegetarian diets, however, do find recipes for filling the meat/egg/dairy void useful. It is that sort of recipe that is given in this section. All are taken from cookbooks listed below; parenthetical numerals after each recipe title refer to the book from which it was taken.

Selected Vegan Cookbooks

Batt, Eva. *'What's Cooking?' A Guide to Good Eating*. Leatherhead, Surrey: The Vegan Society, 1977. (1)

Cottrell, Edyth Young. *The Oats, Peas, Beans, and Barley Cookbook*. Santa Barbara, Calif.: Woodbridge Press, 1974. (2)

Dinshah, Freya. *XXIII World Vegetarian Congress Cookbook*. Malaga, NJ: North American Vegetarian Society, 1975. (3)

—— *The Vegan Kitchen*. Malaga, NJ: American Vegan Society, 1973. (4)

Hurd, Rosalie, and Hurd, Dr Frank. *A Good Cook... Ten Talents*. Chisholm, Minn.: Dr and Mrs F. J. Hurd, 1968. (5)

The Vegan Society. *Practical Veganism*. Enfield, Middlesex: The Vegan Society, 1974. (6)

Also Recommended

Batt, Eva. *What Else is Cooking? Further Adventures in Cooking with Compassion*. Leatherhead, Surrey: The Vegan Society, 1983.

D'Silva, Joyce. *Healthy Eating for the New Age, a Vegan Cookbook:* London: Wildwood House, 1980.

Leneman, Leah. *Vegan Cooking, the Compassionate Way of Eating*. Wellingborough, Northants.: Thorsons, 1982.

World of God, Inc. *The Cookbook for People Who Love Animals*. Umatilla, Fla.: World of God, Inc., 1983.

MAIN DISHES

BUTTER BEAN ROAST (3)

Serves 4

4 oz (115g) dry butter beans
1 pint (570ml) water
1 large onion, diced
1½ teaspoonsful soya flour
1½ teaspoonsful peanut butter
½ teaspoonful pot herbs
Wholemeal breadcrumbs
1 tomato, sliced

1. Soak beans overnight.

2. Add onion. Simmer in the soaking water for about 1 hour and 20 minutes.

3. Drain off water. Mash the beans. Mix in soya flour and peanut butter, then the herbs and breadcrumbs.

4. Oil a loaf tin. Put in layers as follows: half the bean mixture, sliced tomato, and the other half of the bean mixture. Press down well; bake at 400°F/200°C (Gas Mark 6) for 30 minutes.

HI-PROTEIN MILLET PATTIES (5)

2lb (900g) millet, cooked weight
2 oz (55g) nut butter (peanut, almond, cashew, etc.)
1 tablespoonful oil and 1 tablespoonful soya sauce
2 tablespoonsful onion powder
1 teaspoonful sea salt
Celery seeds, rosemary and thyme to taste

1. Mill the ingredients well.

2. Form into patties and brown in lightly oiled pan.

3. Serve with your favourite gravy.

WALNUT-OAT BURGERS (5)

4 oz (115g) oatmeal
4 oz (115g) seasoned breadcrumbs
6 oz (170g) finely chopped onion, sautéed
1 oz (30g) soya flour
2 tablespoonsful cashew nut butter (optional)
Sea salt and sage to taste

1. Mix ingredients well.

2. Add just enough hot water to hold together. Mix well.

3. Brown in oiled frying pan on both sides.

4. Serve in burger buns or with gravy as meatless main dish.

ESAU'S POTTAGE (2)

3 oz (85g) brown rice
1¾ pints (980ml) water
1 teaspoonful sea salt
6 oz (170g) chopped onion, sautéed
2 tablespoonsful oil
½ lb (225g) lentils

1. Add rice to boiling salted water. Cover and let cook 15 minutes.

2. Add onions, oil, and lentils. Boil until lentils are tender; should be mushy.

3. Garnish with parsley and slices of red pepper or pimento.

MUSHROOM AND CASHEW NUT PIE (1)

½lb (225g) cashew nuts
½ pint (285ml) stock or water
1 medium onion
2oz (55g) vegan margarine
½lb (225g) mushrooms
1 tablespoonful wholemeal flour
1 teaspoonful yeast extract
Sea salt

For short-crust pastry:
6oz (170g) wholemeal flour
3oz (85g) vegetable fat
1 tablespoonful cold water

1. Soak the cashew nuts in the water or stock overnight.

2. Make the short-crust pastry by rubbing the fat into the flour until the mixture resembles breadcrumbs. Add sufficient water to make a firm dough, then roll out to cover pie dish.

3. Peel and chop the onion and cook gently in the fat for 10 minutes.

4. Add the mushrooms, washed and roughly chopped, and cook for 5 minutes.

5. Stir in the flour and the nuts with their water. Cover and simmer for 30 minutes, then add the yeast extract and salt.

6. Put into a pie dish and allow to cool before covering with the pastry and baking at 400°F/200°C (Gas Mark 6) for 30 minutes.

7. Serve with lightly cooked vegetables.

THE VEGAN DAIRY

PLAMIL ICE CREAM (1)

½ level teaspoonful agar agar
1 tablespoonful syrup
½ tin of Plamil
1 vanilla pod (or 8 drops vanilla essence)

1. Mix agar with syrup in a pan and add Plamil.

2. Heat gently, almost to boiling, stirring all the time. Have whole vanilla pod therein while cooking or add vanilla essence after taking off the heat.

3. Freeze 2 hours, beating thoroughly after the first hour to prevent crystal formation. Serve with fruit syrup or grated Plamil chocolate.

SESAME/SOYA MILK (4)
Makes 2 pints

3 tablespoonsful sesame seeds
8 pitted dates
¾ pint (425ml) water for soaking
3 tablespoonsful soya flour
1 vanilla pod

1. Soak the sesame seeds and dates for 6 hours. (Sesame seeds may be ground instead.)

2. Add the soya flour and buzz in a blender for about 1½ minutes.

2. Pour into a quart bottle and fill with water nearly to top. Shake.

4. Split the vanilla pod down one side and add it to the liquid.

5. Refrigerate for at least two hours, then remove the vanilla pod – which may be reused several times.

Note: The 'milk' will stay fresh in the refrigerator for up to 2 days.

CASHEW CREAM (4)

2 golden delicious apples
5oz (140g) raw cashews or cashew pieces (cheaper)

1. Peel and dice apples. Buzz in blender with a little water.

2. Add cashews and buzz again. (May need to grind first.)

3. Add more water as needed; the total amount of water is about ½ pint (285ml), but use more or less according to how thick a cream you want.

Note: It is worth blending well to make a smooth cream. Sesame-coconut butter may be used in place of cashews. The cream is delicious on fruit salads, desserts and cereals.

SOYA CHEESE (6)

4oz (115g) hard vegan margarine, e.g. Tomor (UK); Willow Run (US)
1½ teaspoonful yeast extract
3½oz (100g) soya flour

1. Melt margarine in pan, and stir in yeast extract and soya flour. Mix to a smooth paste (soya flour may need sifting).

2. Press into suitable dish and leave to set in cool place.

3. Turn out.

Note: Will keep and cut as cheddar. Other flavouring can be added but may spoil keeping quality and firmness.

PLANTMILK CHEESE (4)

¾ pint (425ml) soya milk
¾ pint (425ml) water
1 teaspoonful ground sesame seeds
Juice of 2 lemons

1. Mix soya milk with water and pour in saucepan.

2. Add sesame seeds and heat to boiling; as mixture begins to rise, pour in juice of lemons.

3. Remove from heat; stir and strain.

4. Put in Kilner/Mason jar with screen lid; place upside-down to drain overnight.

HOT CAROB COCOA (5)

1½ pints (850ml) milk (soya, cashew, coconut, etc.)
3-4 tablespoonsful carob powder
5 pitted dates
Pinch of sea salt
½ teaspoonful vanilla or 1 tablespoonful malt syrup
2 tablespoonsful soya or safflower oil

1. Liquify ingredients until smooth.

2. Add oil slowly and liquify again.

3. Heat but do not boil.

CAROBANANA SHAKE (4)

¾ pint (425ml) sesame/soya or other vegan milk
3 bananas
3 heaped toasted carob

1. Mix together in blender.

INSTEAD OF EGGS

BINDERS (Emulsifiers) (4)

1 teaspoonful arrowroot flour
1 teaspoonful soya flour
6 tablespoonsful (120ml) warm water

1. Mix ingredients.

Note: Mixture is used as a substitute for one egg in conventional recipes. (Another ingredient which can be used as a binder in place of an egg is soya lecithin. Try about ½ teaspoonful per lb of batter for baked items.)

'SCRAMBLED EGGS' (5)

3 tablespoonsful oil
1 tablespoonful onion powder or ½ cupful sautéed fresh
   onion
1 tablespoonful soya sauce
½ teaspoonful sea salt, heaping
¼ teaspoonful turmeric powder
1 lb (455g) crumbled tofu

1. Stir all the ingredients, except for the tofu, together in skillet over medium heat.

2. Add the tofu.

3. Mix well with fork, stirring until seasonings are evenly distributed and mixture heats.

4. Serve like scrambled eggs, with toast.

NO-EGG PANCAKES (1)

4½oz (130g) wholemeal flour
3 rounded tablespoonsful soya flour
Pinch sea salt
⅔ pint (340ml) water
Oil for frying

1. Pour water into blender; switch on and add dry ingredients gradually. Whiz for about 1 minute.

2. Leave in a cool place for at least 1 hour. (Can be left in refrigerator overnight.)

3. Beat again just before using.

Note: If required for fritters use only ⅓ pint (200ml) water. Fry on both sides in very lightly oiled pan and serve while hot with lemon juice and fruit sugar or syrup. (2oz of tofu may be substituted for each egg in traditional pancake recipes.)

FLUFFY EGGLESS SOUFFLÉ (5)

Tomatoes (tinned or fresh)
Water or tomato juice
Soya flour
Onions (fresh or powdered)
4 tablespoonsful oil (for each quart of mixture)
Seasoning: sea salt, sweet basil, onion powder, parsley,
rosemary, garlic or other)

1. Start in blender with tomatoes, adding soya flour gradually, sufficient to make a thick batter.

2. Add oil, onions and seasonings to taste.

3. Pour into ungreased baking dish. Repeat if necessary to make 1½ inches thick.

4. Bake at 425°F/220°C (Gas Mark 7) for 10 minutes.

5. Reduce the heat to low, continue baking 50 minutes.

6. Remove from oven and cover with towel to set.

7. When cooled, cut into squares and serve with salad.

Note: Cold soufflé is delicious mixed with chopped celery and vegan mayonnaise for sandwich filling.

Appendices

The following Appendices offer a pot pourri of vegan companies and organizations, as well as practical information for the would-be vegan. It is certainly not representative of every vegan group in existence but should offer a starting point for anyone seeking products, contacts, and additional facts on this way of life.

Appendix A
The Vegan Society

A group of 'non-dairy vegetarians' separated from the Vegetarian Society (UK) Ltd, to form the Vegan Society in 1944. In the years since, these pioneers and their successors have led the way in making veganism accepted and respected by serving as test cases for research into the effects of their diet on health and by instigating an educational campaign that is constantly growing. This includes the publication and distribution of books and pamphlets, providing speakers for other groups, and manning booths at selected fairs and festivals at which the vegan message might be well received. The BBC film, *A Better Future for All Life*, was made in the mid-1970s under complete direction of the Vegan Society. Its presentation of the vegan lifestyle resulted in 2,000 enquiries during the first week after its airing on British television. Their second film is called *Time for a Change*. The Society publishes a quarterly journal, *The Vegan* and works on specific projects such as current investigation into the establishment of a vegan retirement home. Social events are also frequently planned for members. (See Chapter 2 for the Society's aims.)

The Vegan Society Ltd
47 Highlands Road
Leatherhead, Surrey

Appendix B
The American Vegan Society

The American Vegan Society was founded in 1960 by H. Jay Dinshah, an American, and his wife, Freya Smith Dinshah, from England. Both were lifelong vegetarians. The Society publishes a quarterly tabloid, *Ahimsa*, as well as books and leaflets on the *ahimsa* philosophy, reverence for life, natural living and natural means to health, and vegan food preparation. There is also an annual convention at its New Jersey headquarters, 'Suncrest', which alternately serves as an educational centre at which vacationers can 'learn to live a better life of *ahimsa*, veganism, inner peace, karma yoga, natural hygiene, self-betterment, personal ecology, reverence for life, [and] Gandhian philosophy'. Weekend and week-long cookery courses are also presented, and books on topics related to veganism are available by mail. Seasoned members may serve as 'Vegan Information Points' to offer help to enquirers in local areas.

The American Vegan Society
501 Old Harding Highway
Malaga, NJ 08328
USA

Appendix C
Vegan Views

A delightfully homespun quarterly, *Vegan Views* acts as a forum for readers' opinions, ideas and thoughts, and for their artistic and literary talents, as it seeks to increase communication among vegans. It is an informal periodical that appeals especially to younger people and features such friendly departments as the 'Contacts List' in which new subscribers' names and addresses are given for possible meetings and correspondences.

Recent issues have included articles denouncing drugs (including caffeine, tobacco and sugar), sharing recipes for kitchen cosmetics, and reviewing the offerings of an organized country walks society. Every copy of *Vegan Views* is dotted with poems like the one below, entitled 'Slaughter':

> Who is going to weep
> For the cows and the sheep
> Who's going to cry
> As the slaughterhouse trucks go rolling by
> Are these animals doomed to die?

and reflections such as 'Friends and Relations' in which the writer deals with her relationship with non-vegan loved ones and tacks on the afterthought: 'I considered subtitling this article "How not to feel superior although a vegan"! We vegans can be constantly aware that we are no *better* than other people, just more awakened to the ways . . . we can . . . love.'

Vegans Views
1 Gincroft Lane
Edenfield, Ramsbottom
Bury, Lancs.

Appendix D
Vegfam

The goal of Vegfam is to 'feed the hungry without exploiting animals'. It was begun in 1964 by a vegan couple, Chris and Janet Aldous; he was then a theology student and she a teacher of deaf children, and they made personal expeditions to deliver food to the needy. When family and professional commitments became such that they were obliged to turn the work over to others, Mrs Ruth Howard and her son, Frieden-stern Howard, became the major trustees. As such, they administrate and provide funds for facilitation of the work so that all donations may be routed directly to the cause for which they're earmarked. Today Vegfam often works with and through larger famine relief organizations when they are assured that the aid they're providing on a particular project is in keeping with vegan principles.

One of the most interesting of these is the leaf protein production experiment in India, partially financed by Vegfam. This 'green crop fractionation' involves the extracting of protein from green leaves, abundant in many of the countries where malnutrition and overpopulation are acute problems. A research programme at the Sri Avinashilingham Home College in Southern India involves giving children leaf protein (in this case alfalfa) twice daily in a snack also comprised of maize flour and unrefined sugar; results have been completely favourable.

Other long-term assistance has involved vegetable canning for peasants in North Euboea (Greece); providing seeds for Nigeria, Bangladesh and Ethiopia; irrigation for Uttar Pradesh, Tamil-Nadu and Maharashtra (India), Ethiopia and Lesotho; and fruit and nut trees for Vietnam, Kenya, Mexico, and Canadian Indian reservations. Short-term aid has included the provision of fruit and nuts for Near East refugees and plant-based foodstuffs for children victimized by famine or drought in Bihar and Tamil-Nadu, Nigeria, Vietnam and Bangladesh, plus more recent aid to Cambodia, Sri Lanka and Ethiopia. Among ongoing projects are desert cropping by irrigation, dew conservation, tree planting, etc., conversion of grazing land to food crop acreage, and horticultural training for unemployed youths.

Vegfam
38 Hampden Road
Walsworth
Hitchin, Herts. SG4 0LD

Appendix E
Miscellaneous Organizations

This list, although not exhaustive, gives some indication of the types of societies and charities vegans might support.

Health

The Nature Cure Clinic, 15 Oldbury Place, London W1M 3AL – an outpatient clinic whose three main principles of vegetarianism, nature cure, and anti-vivisection combine to make it unique in Britain. A registered charity.

The Community Health Foundation, East-West Centre, 188-194 Old Street, London EC1V 9BD – offers courses in holistic living, natural healing, nutrition, yoga, Shiatsu massage, health education, preventative medicine. Food is macrobiotic. A registered charity.

Animal Welfare

Animal Aid, 7 Castle Street, Tonbridge, Kent TN9 1BH – campaigns against all animal cruelty, specifically against animal experiments and factory farming. Publishes *Outrage*, a bi-monthly newsletter.

Beauty Without Cruelty Charitable Trust, 11 Limehill Road, Tunbridge Wells, Kent – established in 1959 by Muriel, the Lady Dowding, as an educational society concerned with animal abuse in furs and other clothing and in cosmetics. Although Lady Dowding is no longer affiliated with BWC, much information about its history and philosophy is found in her autobiography *Beauty – Not the Beast*, published by Neville Spearman. Separate from the charity but spawned by the need which the charity saw is Beauty Without Cruelty Ltd, Tonbridge, Kent, a cosmetic firm whose products are not tested on animals and which are vegetarian (although not all vegan) in content.

Captive Animals' Protection Society, 17 Raphael Road, Hove, East Sussex BN3 5QP – especially concerned with the use of performing animals; campaigns against their inclusion in circuses.

Compassion in World Farming, 20 Lavant Street, Petersfield, Hants. GU32 3EW – campaigns against violence in agriculture, be it directed towards animals, the soil, plants or man; its work is centred against livestock production by intensive means. Its magazine is *Ag*. A similar group in the US is *FARM* (Farm Animal Reform Movement), P.O. Box 70123, Washington, DC 20088.

Dr Hadwen Trust for Humane Research, Tylers Way, Watford, Herts. WD2 8HQ – promotes the development of humane alternatives to live animal experiments by funding non-animal medical and scientific research and by educational literature. Quarterly newsletter: *Alternative News*.

Friends of the Earth, 377 City Road, London EC1V 1NA – concerned with wildlife and ecological issues such as pollution, conservation, energy, etc. Bulletin is issued six times yearly.

League Against Cruel Sports, 83-87 Union Street, London SE1 1SG – works to oppose hunting of all animals and buys land to create sanctuaries where hunting is prohibited. Magazine: *Cruel Sports*.

Vegetarianism

Friends Vegetarian Society, c/o Tom Haley, Librarian, 69 Oakwood Crescent, London N21 1PA – established in 1902 by a group of Friends (Quakers) who practised vegetarianism as part of their religious convictions; aims to assist members of the Religious Society of Friends and other people to follow a vegetarian way of life. Several meetings in London each year. Members from throughout the world receive periodic newsletters. Registered charity. (An offshoot formed in North America in 1982: Box 474, Beverly, MA 01915.)

International Jewish Vegetarian Society, Bet Teva, 853-855 Finchley Road, London NW11 8LX – founded in 1964 and aiming to make known Jewish teachings in which a non-carnivorous way of life is advocated. Emphasizes that the eating of animals involves the individual in 'cruel and obscene traffic' and promotes living on pure, wholefood products. Its membership quarterly is *The Jewish Vegetarian*.

The Vegetarian Society of the UK Ltd, Parkdale, Dunham Road, Altrincham, Cheshire WA14 4QG; London Information Centre: 53 Marloes Road, Kensington, London W8 6LA – formed in 1969 through the amalgamation of two older organizations, the Vegetarian Society and the London Vegetarian Society. An educational body and registered charity endeavouring to impart knowledge of the benefits of a vegetarian diet in terms of ethics, health, economics, ecology and reduction of famine in the Third World. Bimonthly journal: *The Vegetarian*.

Vegetarian Children's and Elderly Persons' Homes

Jersey Vegetarian Home for Children, Hon. Secretary Mrs E. Flack, 'Quarrywood', 23 Grange Road, Hastings, East Sussex.

Homes for Elderly Vegetarians Ltd, 159 Clapham High Street, London SW4 7SS, has homes in East and West Sussex, Yorkshire and North Wales.

The Abbeyfield Edinburgh Society Ltd runs a retirement home for vegetarians at 42 Cacaan Lane, Edinburgh, EH10 4SU, Scotland.

The Beulah Trust, c/o The Secretary, Miss R. Bennett, The Green, Snelsmore House, Newbury, Berks., is a charity aiming to set up homes for frail vegetarians *and vegans*.

Appendix F
The Farm

Established in 1971 by Stephen Gaskin, The Farm, now a working community of 500, has a spiritual basis and veganism inherent in its lifestyle. Most Farm inhabitants lived formerly in households of up to thirty persons, although single-family residences are now more popular. Their veganism is for 'ecological, moral, spiritual and health reasons, primarily spiritual and moral', according to Rob Denton, a salesman for Farm Foods, one of the businesses affording the community its self-sufficiency. Farm Foods manufactures soya milk, tofu and tempeh for Farm members' consumption, and tempeh starter, tempeh-making kits, and a frozen soya dessert, 'Ice Bean', for distribution throughout North America. They wholesale, but do not produce, a textured vegetable protein and a 'Good-Tasting Nutritional Yeast'. Another venture, the Book Publishing Company, has published titles including *This Season's People* (vignettes of Farm philosophy from Stephen Gaskin), *The Farm Vegetarian Cookbook*, and *Spiritual Midwifery*, detailing the natural childbirth carried out there with such success that women actually move to The Farm temporarily that they might experience their pregnancy and delivery under the care of Ina May Gaskin and other skilled Farm midwives. Another project is 'Flower Power', a non-violent electronic game.

Expanding from their Tennessee headquarters, there is a rural Farm in Ontario and an affiliated 'soy dairy' in Eire; a city centre in the South Bronx area of New York City and another in Washington, DC; and relief efforts in Guatemala, and Lesotho, Africa. They also run ambulance services for the urban poor. 'We're not evangelistic, though,' says Denton. 'We just try to set an example and work for peaceful, non-violent change.'

Because they believe that God inspired all religions,

We honour the major old religions, like Christianity, Judaism, and Buddhism . . . We should love one another, not be rich, and our lives should show that we're living our religion every day. That's why we're vegan and non-violent and not rich! We're non-denominational; it's the same religion that's been on earth for thousands of years: every generation expresses it in a different way, and we're expressing it our way.

After thirteen years of total dietary veganism, the Farm policy now allows the choice of lacto-vegetarianism and many of its members now use dairy products. The leaders remain staunchly vegan.

The Farm
Summertown, Tenn. 38488
USA

Appendix G
Plamil Foods Ltd

To develop a palatable vegan 'milk' was a priority of the Vegan Society from shortly after its inception in 1944. Vegans gathered even then to attempt to meet the desire of their confrères for a milk-like product that could be used in tea, coffee and cooking, and would assist in weaning infants. Health food companies had said that there was insufficient demand for such a product so the vegans themselves formed a company to formulate and ultimately to manufacture it. 'We didn't do market research,' said Plamil president Arthur Ling. 'We just thought the demand would come as people were educated.' Although it was not until 1965 that the tasty liquid 'Plantmilk' (now 'Plamil') was marketed, the product is now holding its own on the British health food market, despite the fact that the heavily subsidized dairy industry makes Plamil completely non-competitive with cow's milk when prices are compared.

The company, now staffed almost entirely by vegans, has its plant and offices in what was formerly a small, conventional dairy. Expansion has given rise to a cream ('Delice'), a 'chocolate milk' ('Carob-ean'), and a rice pudding. Hopes for a commercial vegan cheese are high but the resources for its development have not been available to date. To have a Plamil cheese, though, is a definite, albeit long-range, goal for Arthur Ling, whose association with the company has primed him for long-term planning:

When Plamil started, it was an act of faith. I worked at it part-time. It was a constant headache initially. One health food proprietor said, 'You're ahead of your time,' but later he became a shareholder. All the shareholders sustained losses at first, but they weren't investing to make money. They invested because they believed in it and if you're determined you're going to win, you will.

Plamil Foods Ltd
Plamil House
Bowles Well Gardens
Folkestone, Kent

Appendix H
Jane Howard Cosmetics

A totally vegan line of skin care products is that of Jane Howard Cosmetics which, in the words of Ms Howard, 'hiccoughed its way into existence in June of 1980'. In search of quality products for her own sensitive skin, the company's founder – formerly a bacteriologist in a milk-testing laboratory – suspected animal products and petrochemicals as the primary complexion foes. Her line contains neither of these and is also without artificial colourings. What *is* included is listed fully on every label so that someone allergic even to some natural ingredients can choose wisely.

A vegetarian and associate member of the Vegan Society, Jane Howard markets her products without their having been tested on animals. 'We test on ourselves, on a panel of people with different skin types. We also do periodic shelf tests to see that the products remain pure. It's rather amazing: they don't rot.' (The preservative used is based on synthetic vitamin C.)

The line includes cleansers, beauty grains, day and night moisturizers, an after-shave balm for men, and a variety of hand treatments and body oils. Jane Howard Cosmetics are sold in health food shops throughout Great Britain.

Jane Howard Ltd
The Cottage
49 Springfield Street
Barnsley, South Yorkshire

Note: There are cosmetics and toiletries for vegans in other product lines as well. Information may be obtained in the UK in *The Vegan* or from the Beauty Without Cruelty Charitable Trust, (see Appendix E). In the US, comprehensive lists of suitable products are available from the BWC Charity, 175 W. 12th., New York, NY 10011, and by ordering a back issue of *Ahimsa* (July – Sept. 1984) from the American Vegan Society, (see Appendix B). Send $2 for either of these.

Reference Bibliography

1: Books and Pamphlets

Altman, Nathaniel. *Eating for Life*, with a preface by Geoffrey Hodson, rev. edn, Wheaton, Ill.: Quest Books, Theosophical Publishing House, 1977.

Bargen, Richard, M.D. *The Vegetarian's Self-Defense Manual.* Wheaton, Ill.: Quest Books, Theosophical Publishing House, 1979.

Batt, Eva. *Why Veganism?* Malaga, NJ: American Vegan Society, n.d.

——*Wool Factories.* Leatherhead, Surrey: The Vegan Society, n.d.

Clark, Stephen R. L. *The Moral Status of Animals.* Oxford: Oxford University Press, 1977.

Dinshah, H. Jay, ed. *Here's Harmlessness.* Malaga, NJ: American Vegan Society, 1973.

—— *How to Be a Total-Vegetarian.* Malaga, NJ: American Vegan Society, 1975.

—— *Out of the Jungle*, 4th edn. Malaga, NJ: American Vegan Society, 1975.

Dorland's Medical Dictionary, 24th edn. S.v. 'Vegan'.

Fox, Michael W., M.D., Ph.D., D.V.M. 'What Future for Man and Earth? Toward a Biospiritual Ethic'. In *On the Fifth Day: Animal Rights and Human Ethics*. Richard Knowles Morris and Michael W. Fox, eds. Washington, DC: Acropolis Books, 1978. (British distributor: Springwood Books), pp.219-30.

Freeman, Dan. *The Great Apes.* New York: G. P. Putnam's Sons, 1979.

Giehl, Dudley. *Vegetarianism, a Way of Life*, with a foreword by Isaac Bashevis Singer. New York: Harper & Row, 1979. (British distributor: MacDonald and Evans, Ltd.)

Gregory, Richard Claxton. *Dick Gregory's Natural Diet for Folks Who Eat: Cookin' With Mother Nature.* New York: Perennial Library, 1974. (British distributor: Thorsons Ltd.)

Hamilton, Clarence H., ed. *Buddhism: A Religion of Infinite Compassion, Selections from Buddhist Literature.* Indianapolis: Bobbs-Merrill, 1952. (British distributor: Eurospan Ltd.)

Hardon, John A., S.J. *Religions of the Orient, A Christian View.* Chicago: Loyola University Press, 1970.

Harris, John. *Vegetarianism: The Ethics*. Altrincham, Cheshire: The Vegetarian Society (UK), 1978.

Harrison, Ruth. *Animal Machines*. London: Vincent Stuart, 1964.

[Hershaft, Alex.] *Vegetarianism Like It Is*. Washington, DC: Vegetarian-Information Services, n.d.

Holmes-Gore, Revd V. A. *These We Have Not Loved: A Treatise on the Christian Attitude to the Creatures*. London: C. D. Daniel, 1941.

[Jannaway, Kathleen.] *What Happens to the Calf?* Leatherhead, Surrey: The Vegan Society, 1975.

Joy, Charles R., trans. and ed. *The Animal World of Albert Schweitzer: Jungle Insights into Reverence for Life*. Boston: Beacon Press, 1950. (British distributor: Harper & Row Ltd.)

Kovik, James, and Mary Jo Kovik. *The True Facts on Slaughter for Sport*. Baltimore: Defenders of Animal Rights, 1977.

Langley, Gill. *Animals and Cosmetics – What Is the Connection?* London: British Union for the Abolition of Vivisection, 1980.

Lappé, Frances Moore. *Diet For a Small Planet*, rev. edn. New York: Balantine Books, 1975. (British distributor: MacDonald and Co. [Publishers] Ltd.)

Linzey, Andrew. 'Animals in Moral Theology (1)'. In *Animal Rights – a Symposium*. David Paterson and Richard D. Ryder, eds. Fontwell, Sussex: Centaur Press, 1979, pp.34-42.

Lucas, Jack. *Vegetarianism: The World Food Problem*. Altrincham, Cheshire: the Vegetarian Society (UK), 1978.

Noss, John B. *Man's Religions*, 6th rev. edn. West Drayton, Middlesex: Collier Macmillan Ltd, 1980.

Osborn, Marjorie. *More than Skin Deep*. Tunbridge Wells, Kent: Beauty Without Cruelty, 1975.

Prabhavananda, Swami, and Christopher Isherwood, trans. and eds. *How to Know God, The Yoga Aphorisms of Patanjali*. Hollywood: Vedanta Press, 1953. (British distributor: Ramakrishna Vedanta Centre.)

—— *The Song of God, Bhagavad-Gita*. New York: New American Library, 1972. (British distribution: New English Library Ltd.)

Regan, Tom, and Peter Singers, eds. *Animal Rights and Human Obligations*. Hemel Hempstead, Herts: Prentice-Hall, 1976.

Sanders, T. A. B., and Frey R. Ellis. *Vegan Nutrition*. Leatherhead, Surrey: The Vegan Society, 1979.

Schweitzer, Albert. 'The Ethic of Reverence for Life'. In Regan, *Animal Rights and Human Obligations*. Hemel Hempstead, Herts. Prentice-Hall, 1976, pp.133-8.

Singer, Peter. *Animal Liberation: A New Ethics in Our Treatment of Animals*. Wellingborough, Northants.: Thorsons, 1983.

Sussman, Vic. *The Vegetarian Alternative: A Guide to a Healthful and Humane Diet*. Emmaus, Pa.: Rodale Press, 1978.

Turnbill, Eric. 'Animals in Moral Theology (2)'. In *Animal Rights – a*

Symposium. David Paterson and Richard D. Ryder, eds. Fontwell, Sussex: Centaur Press: 1979, pp.43-7.

Vyvyan, John. *In Pity and in Anger: A Study of the Use of Animals in Science*. London: Michael Joseph: 1969.

—— *The Dark Face of Science*. London: Michael Joseph, 1971.

Vegan Society, The, *Food for a Future*. Leatherhead, Surrey: The Vegan Society, n.d.

Wynne-Tyson, Jon. *Food for a Future, The Complete Case for Vegetarianism*. London: Centaur Press, 1979.

Yogananda, Paramahansa. *Autobiography of a Yogi*, 14th edn. Los Angeles: Self-Realization Fellowship, 1971.

II: Periodical Articles and Other Resources

Allanson, Rob. 'Cutting Through the Cream Cheese'. *East-West Journal*, June 1980, pp.51-8.

Bonnie, Harry. ['Letters to the Editor'] *The Vegan* XVI (Summer 1969): 26.

Bowden, Mark. 'The Modern Test-Tube Cow'. *East-West Journal*, June 1980, pp.31-5.

Braunstein, Mark. 'On Being Radically Vegetarian'. *Vegetarian Times*, March 1980, pp. 72-3.

Coles, Serena. 'Blueprint for a Humane World'. Paper presented at the 23rd World Vegetarian Congress, University of Maine at Orono, 18 August, 1975.

—— ['Letters to the Editor'] *The Vegan* XVI (Summer 1969): 26.

'Diet and Stress in Vascular Disease'. In *Journal of the American Medical Association*. 179 (9) (1961): 806-7.

Henderson, G. Allan. 'The Four Pillars of Health'. *The Vegan* III (Spring 1947): 1.

Hicks, Jo, and John Hicks. 'Why *We're* Vegan'. *The Vegan* XXVI (Summer 1979): 30.

Jackson, Jon A. 'The Life and Death of an American Chicken'. *Saturday Review*, 2 September, 1974, pp.12-13.

Kellert, Stephen. 'Attitudes Towards Animals'. *Vegetarian Times*, Sept.-Oct. 1978, pp.15-24.

Mason, James B. 'Industrial Pigs, Mechanical Chickens: How Corporate Animal Factories Breed Poisoned Meat and New Pollution'. *Vegetarian Times*, March 1980, pp.52-3.

Moran, Patrick K. 'Vegetarianism and the Cardio-Vascular System'.

Master's thesis. University of Missouri at Kansas City, 1975.

Moran, Victoria M. 'The Self-Healing Body: A Look at the Theory of Natural Hygiene.' *Vegetarian Times*, July 1980, pp.51-3.

Nutritional Perspectives III (April 1980), back cover.

Rajneesh, Bhagwan Shree. 'The Spiritual Side of Vegetarianism'. *Vegetarian Times*, March 1980, pp.64-5.

Study Circle for Animal Welfare (Irish Catholic branch). 'Annual Report'. Dublin: Irish Catholic Study Circle for Animal Welfare, 1979.

Vegan Society, The, *A Better Future for All Life*. In film series 'The Open Door'. London: British Broadcasting Corpn, n.d.

Whitaker, Julian, M.D. 'Vegan Diet in Cardio-Vascular Disease Therapy'. Address presented at the North American Vegetarian Society Annual Conference, Earlham College, Richmond, Ind., 12 July, 1980.

'You Are What You Eat'. In *East-West Journal*, June 1980, p.13.

III. Additional Recommended Reading

Akers, Keith. *A Vegetarian Sourcebook*. New York: G. P. Putnam's Sons, 1983. ('Provides solid scientific arguments on nutrition and refutes protein complementary theory; also delves into impact of meat-eating on environment, agriculture, society' – from Scott Smith, *Vegetarian Times*, P.O. Box 570, Oak Park, Ill. 60603, USA.)

Altman, Nathaniel. *Ahimsa (Dynamic Compassion)*. Wheaton, Ill.: Quest Books, Theosophical Publishing House, 1980. (An anthology from noted exponents of non-violence; deals with *ahmisa* among people, towards animals, the environment, etc.)

— — *Total Vegetarian Cooking, What You Need to Know*. 36 Grove St, New Canaan, Connecticut 06840: Keats Publishing Co., 1981. (Includes menus for both lacto-ovo-vegetarians and vegans, and for the special needs of children, pregnant women, athletes and slimmers.)

Berry, Rynn, Jun. *The Vegetarians*. Brookline, Massachusetts: Autumn Press, 1979. (Fourteen famous men and women tell why they turned to vegetarianism; among them are: Isaac Bashevis Singer; Dr Gordon Latto; Dr Alan Long; Brigid Brophy; Muriel, the Lady Dowding; and Malcolm Muggeridge.)

Clark, Stephen R. L. *The Nature of the Beast: Are Animals Moral?* London: Oxford University Press, 1982. (Ethical treatise by vegan philosopher and animal rights activist.)

Cook, John. *Diet and Your Religion*. Santa Barbara, Calif.: Woodbridge Press, 1976. (Offers advice for better health from the world's religions. British distributor: Thorsons.)

Godlovitch, Stanley, Rosalind Godlovitch, and John Harris, eds. *Animals, Men and Morals*. New York: Grove Press, 1971. (An 'inquiry into the maltreatment of non-humans' collected by three British philosophers and including contributions from: Ruth Harrison; Richard Ryder; Muriel, the Lady Dowding; and others. British distributor: Transatlantic Book Service Ltd.)

Hur, Robin. *Food Reform, Our Desperate Need*. 3707 Kerbey Lane, Austin, Texas 78731: Heidelberg Publishers, 1975. (Propounds simple diet of raw foods, sprouts, etc. for vigorous health.)

Kapleau, Philip. *To Cherish All Life*. London: Rider, 1983. (A Zen Buddhist view of animal slaughter and case for vegetarianism.)

Regan, Tom. *All That Dwell Therein*. Berkeley: University of California Press, 1982. (Philosophical exploration of animals' rights and environmental ethics. British distributor: C.C.J. Ltd, London.)

Reusch, Hans. *Slaughter of the Innocent*. New York: Bantam Books, 1978. (Modern classic of the anti-vivisection cause.)

Ryder, Richard. *Victims of Science*. London: Centaur Press, 1983. (More on vivisection from a clinical psychologist whose professional training introduced him to the laboratory environment firsthand.)

Salt, Henry S. *Animals' Rights*. London: Centaur Press, 1980. (Pioneering thesis on our obligations to other species.)

Wynne-Tyson, Jon, ed. *The Extended Circle*. London: Centaur Press, 1984. (Anthology chronicling the indivisibility of violence.)

Index

ahimsa, 15, 26, 27-8, 30-2, 108
Ahimsa (journal), 15, 118
Aldous, Chris & Janet, 110
Allanson, Rob, 85 (n 14)
allergies, 87, 89, 119
Altman, Nathaniel, 78, (n 3), 79 (n 10), 80 (n 6, 7, 8), 81 (n 8), 82 (n 11), 84 (n 4), 85 (n 4, 8, 9, 13, 16)
Altschul, Aaron, 81 (n 10)
Amer. Med. Assn., Journal of the, 67
Amer. Vegan Soc., 15, 16, 20, 74, 76 (n 8), 108
Amory, Cleveland, 79-80 (n 17)
amino acids. *See* protein
animals, abuses of, 38-9, 52; attitudes towards, 35-6; laboratory tests on, 17, 59, 70, 72, 75-6 (n 5); number saved by vegetarian, 38; telepathic communication with, 86 (n 9); vegetarians' attitude toward, 35, 36. *See also* farming, factory; pets; reverence for life; wildlife: vivisection
animal foods, health hazards of, 17, 67; inefficiency of, 46-7; land use in, 46. *See also* eggs; honey; hunger (famine); meat; milk; pesticide levels
Aquinas, Thomas, 24-5
athletes, vegan/vegetarian, 69

B_{12}, vitamin, 64-5, 87, 89
Baker, Richard St. Barbe, 48
Batt, Eva, 19, 81 (n 15), 83 (n 14)
Beauty Without Cruelty Charitable Trust, 58, 112, 119-20
Beauty Without Cruelty, Ltd. *See* cosmetics
Bean, Louis H., 47
Bentham, Jeremy, 9
Bhagavad-Gita. See Hindu(ism)
Bible, The, 22, 23, 25
Bland, Harold and Jenny, 48-9
Boerma, Addeke H., 45
Bonnie, Harry, 69, 85 (n 18)
Bowden, Mark, 78 (n 19)
Brambell Report, 40-1, 43
Braunstein, Mark, 81 (n 14)
breastfeeding (nursing), 63, 88, 89
Brophy, Brigid, 39
Brown, Lester, 82 (n 14)
Buddhism, 29-30. *See also* religions, Eastern
Buyukmihci, Hope and Gavit, 36

calcium, 63-4, 66, 87, 88
carbohydrates (starches), complex (natural), 63, 91; refined, 54, 63, 92. *See also* grain
carob, 83 (n 7), 115; recipes using, 103
cereal, vegan toppings for, 83 (n 10). *See also* milk, non-dairy; muesli; recipes, vegan dairy substitutes
Catholic(ism), 24, 25-6; Study Circle for Animal Welfare, 25, 26. *See also* Aquinas, Thomas; Bible, The; Christianity; Saori, Fr. Padraic O.; Teilhard de Chardin
cheese, 29, 40, 41, 53, 64. *See also* cheeses, vegan; milk; veal
cheeses, vegan, 54-5, 56, 117, 192. *See also* tofu
chickens, battery. *See* eggs, production
children, vegan/vegetarian, 87-90 passim; books on rearing, 90; home for, 114
cholesterol, 63. *See also* fats
Christianity, 14, 20-6 passim, 30, 33. *See also* Bible, The; Catholic(ism); Friends, Relig. Soc. of; Jesus; Lawson, Margaret
Cinqué, Dr Ralph, 84 (n 2)
Clark, Dr Stephen R. L., 14, 51-2
Coles, Serena, 66, 82 (n 13), 85 (n 19)
commodities, vegan, 18, 53, 57-60
cookbooks, recommended, 90, 96, 97-8
cosmetics, 16, 58-60; Beauty Without Cruelty, Ltd., 58-9, 60, 112; Jane Howard, Ltd., 59-60, 119; in US, 119-20; testing of, 58-9, 75-6 (n 5); 117, 119. *See also* animals, laboratory tests on; vivisection
Compassion in World Farming, 31, 113
cost (of vegan food), 84 (n 18)

Déscartes, René, 37
Denton, Rob, 115-16
Diet for a Small Planet. See Lappé, Frances Moore
Dinshah, H. Jay, 30-2, 54, 77 (n 1)
Dowding, The Lady Muriel, 86 (n 23), 112
Draize test. *See* animals, laboratory tests on; cosmetics, testing of; vivisection
drugs, 11, 13, 16, 57, 70, 88

eating out, 54, 55. *See also* veganism, social considerations of ecology, 35, 48-50 passim, 73, 113
Edison, Thomas, 71

eggs, 17, 39, 40, 53; free-range, 43, 54; production, 41-3; substitutes 82-3 (n 6), 103-5
Ellis, Dr Frey, 70, 84 (n 5)
Essenes, 23

Farm, The, 25, 48, 115-16
farming, factory, 16, 39-44 passim, 113
fats, 63, 67, 91
Fellowship of Life, 21, 22
fibre, 63, 91
film, photographic, 72
fish, eating of, 23, 39, 46, 52, 54. See also fishing
fishing, 13, 39, 57. See also fish, eating of
food groups, four, 61-2
formulas, infant, 88
Fox, Dr Michael, 73-4
Friends, Relig. Soc. of (Quakers), 15, 23, 24, 113
fur(s), 16, 57, 112

Gandhi, Mohandas K., 15, 26, 27-8, 33, 108
gardening, 48, 49, 72, 82 (n 20)
Gaskin, Stephen, 25, 115. See also Farm, The
Giehl, Dudley, 77 (n 10)
Goodall, Jane, 37-8
grain, fed to farm animals, 46; in vegan diet, 48, 55, 56-7, 60-3 passim, 89, 92; recipes using, 94, 98-9, 104
Gregory, Dick, 33

Hardinge, Dr Mervyn G., 68-9
Hardon, John, 30
Harris, John, 80 (n 2)
healing, systems of, 70-1
health, holistic, 9-11, 66-72 passim; foods, 54, 57; organizations, 112; spiritual component of, 11. See also healing, systems of; nature cure; veganism, health benefits of; vegans, health of; vegetarianism, health benefits of
Hershaft, Alex, 75 (n 2), 84 (n 1)
Hicks, Jo and John, 82 (n 4)
Hindu(ism), 26, 28. See also Gandhi, Mohandas K.; religions, Eastern; Yoga Sutras, Patanjali's
Holmes-Gore, Revd V. A., 24
honey, 18, 58, 76 (n 10), 92
Howard, Friedenstern, 110
Howard, Ruth, 36, 110
Hugo, Victor, 34
hunger (famine), 45-7, 73, 75 (n 3), 110-11, 115. See also animal foods, inefficiency of; Vegfam
Hunt, K. E., 81 (n 7)
hunting, 16, 57, 113. See also shooting

iron, 63-4, 87, 88

Jainism, 28-9. See also religions, Eastern
Jannaway, Kathleen, 15, 23, 77 (n 13), 81 (n 16, 18)
Jesus, 21, 23-4, 34. See also Christianity
Judaism, 22, 59, 113. See also prophets, Hebrew

Jung, Dr Carl, 70

Kellert, Dr Stephen, 35-6
King, Dr Martin Luther, Jr., 33
Kingsford, Dr Anna, 26
Kovik, James and Mary Jo, 80 (n 13)

lactose intolerance, 69
Langley, Chris, 72
Langley, Gill, 72, 75-6 (n 5), 84 (n 16)
Lappé, Frances Moore, 45, 47, 54, 62, 87-8
Lawson, Margaret, 21-2, 23, 24
laws, animal protection, 43; product labelling, 57, 58
leather, 17, 29, 40, 49, 57, 60, 72
legumes (pulses), 61, 62, 64, 87, 88, 89, 92; recipe using, 98
Ling, Arthur, 44, 117-18
Linzey, Andrew, 77 (n 9)

margarines, vegan, 60; vitamin D in, 65
Mason, James B., 80 (n 11)
meat, eliminating, 54; hormones in, 67-8; hygienic objections to, 68. See also animal foods; animals, abuses of; veal; veganism; vegetarianism menus, vegan, 56-7
muesli, 56, 83 (n 8). See also cereal, vegan toppings for
milk, 26, 29, 39, 40, 52, 64; production of, 40-1; non-dairy, 26, 27, 44, 55, 65, 83 (n 10), 87, 88, 115, 117-18; respiratory complaints with dairy, 69. See also animal foods; cheese; cheeses, vegan; farming, factory; veal; veganism
minerals, 63-4
miso, 56, 82 (n 5)
Moran, Patrick, 17, 85 (n 12)

Natural Hygiene, 17, 71, 108
Nature Cure, 69, 70, 112
non-violence. See Gandhi, Mohandas K.; King, Dr Martin Luther, Jr.; pacifism; Peace Pilgrim; peace, world; veganism
Noss, John, 78 (n 10, 23)
North Amer. Vegetarian Soc., 44
nuts, 54, 55, 57, 60, 61, 64, 87, 92, 97; recipes using, 96, 99, 100, 102, 103

organizations, animal welfare/rights, 112-13; health, 112; vegetarian, 113-14
Osborn, Marjorie, 83 (n 15), 84 (n 17)
Overeaters Anonymous, 93
overweight (obesity), 69, 87, 92. See also slimming

pacifism, 15, 21. See also Friends, Relig. Soc. of; Gandhi, Mohandas K.; King, Dr Martin Luther, Jr.; Peace Pilgrim; peace, world; veganism
Paul, Saint, 25
Peace Pilgrim, 73, 74
peace, world, 50-1, 52, 73
pesticide levels, in animal foods, 68; in mother's milk, 88
pets, 35-6, 37; feeding, 17, 60, 79 (n 16)
physiology, human and ape compared, 37-8

Plamil, 101, 102, 117-18. *See also* Ling, Arthur; milk, non-dairy

plants, life in, 49-50

pregnancy, 63, 88

Preston, Dr T. R., 80 (n 10)

protein, 62-3, 64, 90; calories in, 91; for children, 87-8; complementarity, 62; leaf 110. *See also* Cinque, Dr Ralph; food groups, four; Lappé, Frances Moore; Whitaker, Dr Julian

prophets, Hebrew, 22-3. *See also* Bible, The

pulses. *See* legumes

Quakers. *See* Friends, Relig. Soc. of

Rajneesh, Bhagwan Shree, 78 (n 16)

recipes, egg replacements, 103-05; low calorie, 93-6; main dish, 98-100; dairy replacements, 101-03

Regan, Tom, 80 (n 1)

religion (and vegans), 14-15, 78 (n 12), 116; religions, Eastern, 15, 26, 27, 28-30; suggesting vegetarianism, 25-6, 30, 31

rennet. *See* cheese

restaurants. *See* eating out

retirement homes, vegetarian/vegan, 109, 114

reverence for life, 18, 20, 21, 25, 90, 108. *See also* Schweitzer, Dr Albert; veganism; vegetarianism

Roberts, Dr Catherine, 11

Roberts, Peter. *See* Compassion in World Farming

Saori, Fr Padraic O., 25

St Barbe Baker, Richard. *See* Baker, Richard St. Barbe

Sanders, T. A. B., 84 (n 5)

Sanderson, Jack, 44, 51

Schweitzer, Dr Albert, 14, 20-1

seaweeds, 64

Shamberger, Dr Raymond, 67

Shaw, George Bernard, 51

Shelley, Percy B., 34

shooting, 39-40, 80 (n 13). *See also* hunting

silk, 13, 57-8

Singer, Peter, 53, 75 (n 1), 80 (n 1, 9), 81 (n 17, 23)

slaughter, 30, 38

slimming, 69, 90-6 passim. *See also* overweight (obesity)

Smith, A. D. M., 84 (n 6)

soaps, vegan, 59. *See also* cosmetics

soya. *See* legumes (pulses); milk, non-dairy; tempeh; tofu

spirituality, 10, 32, 73. *See also* Christianity; religion (and vegans); religions, Eastern; veganism, spiritual aspects of

Stevens, Henry Bailey, 50

sugar(s), 54, 89, 92, 109, 110

Sussman, Vic, 81 (n 1), 85 (n 5, 6)

Teilhard de Chardin, Pierre, 15, 22

Textured vegetable protein (TVP), 61, 92, 115

Thoreau, Henry David, 15, 34

tempeh, 65

tofu, 82-3 (n 6), 87, 88, 92, 104; recipes using, 93, 94, 95, 104

Tolstoy, Ct. Leo, 34, 71

trees, 47-8, 111

Turnbill, Eric, 77 (n 11)

veal, 40-1. *See also* farming, factory; milk production

Vegan, The, 18, 54, 58, 70, 86 (n 24), 87, 119

veganism, adopting, 53-60; compared with vegetarianism, 16-7, 40, 43-4, 53; defined/ explained, 13, 16, 19; health benefits of 14, 69; medical views on, 16, 17, 57, 67, 68-9, 70; social considerations of 18, 55, 89; spiritual aspects of, 14, 69-70, 74; stand of, 37-44 passim. *See also Vegan, The*; Vegan Society, The; vegans

Vegan Society, The, 15, 74, 76 (n 8), 82 (n 17), 89-90, 117; appendix on, 107; on commodities, 57, 119; dietary **recommendations** of, 87; objectives of, **18-19**

Vegan Views, 109

vegans, descriptions of, 13-14, 15, 72; health of, 68; number of, 86 (n 24). *See also* veganism

vegetables, green (leafy), 61, 87, 89, 92

Vegetarian Society, The, 107, 113-14

vegetarianism, basic premise, 37; defined, 16; ethical, 16-17, 32, 38, 74; health benefits of, 36, 67; spiritual aspects of, 14, 30. *See also* veganism, compared with vegetarianism

vegetarians, famous, 34; viewed by vegans, 44

Vegfam, 110

vitamin B_{12}. *See* B_{12}, vitamin

vitamins, **64-6**, 87, 88, 89

vivisection, 16, 21, 41; alternatives to, 75-6 (n 5), 113. *See also* animals, laboratory tests on; cosmetics, testing of; drugs

war, 50-1, 72. *See also* pacifism; peace, world

Watson, Donald, 16

Whitaker, Dr Julian, 57, 84 (n 3)

Wilcox, Ella Wheeler, 34

wildlife, 35-6, 39, 40; organizations, 40, 113; preserves, 36, 47. *See also* hunting; fur(s); shooting

wool, 13, 57, 58

Wynne-Tyson, Jon, 9-11, 35, 79 (n 12), 81 (n 9)

yeast extracts, 56, 60, 65, 83, 88. *See also* B_{12}, vitamin

Yoga Sutras, Patanjali's, 28-9

Yogananda, Paramanhansa, 77 (n4), 78 (n 9)